Metacognitive therapy is based on the principle that worry and rumination are universal processes leading to emotional disorder. These processes are linked to erroneous beliefs about thinking and unhelpful self-regulation strategies.

*Metacognitive Therapy: Distinctive Features* is an introduction to the theoretical foundations and therapeutic principles of metacognitive therapy. Divided into two parts, *Theory* and *Practice*, and using 30 key points, the authors explore how metacognitive therapy can allow people to escape from repetitive thinking patterns that often lead to prolonged psychological distress.

This book is a valuable resource for both students and practitioners wishing to develop a basic understanding of metacognitive therapy and how it compares and contrasts with traditional forms of cognitive-behavioural therapy.

**Peter Fisher** is a Lecturer in Clinical Psychology at the University of Liverpool and a Clinical Psychologist with Manchester Mental Health and Social Care Trust.

**Adrian Wells** is Professor of Clinical and Experimental Psychopathology at the University of Manchester and Professor II in Clinical Psychology at Norwegian University, Trondheim.

Cognitive-behavioural therapy (CBT) occupies a central position in the move towards evidence-based practice and is frequently used in the clinical environment. Yet there is no one universal approach to CBT and clinicians speak of first-, second-, and even third-wave approaches.

This series provides straightforward, accessible guides to a number of CBT methods, clarifying the distinctive features of each approach. The series editor, Windy Dryden, successfully brings together experts from each discipline to summarise the 30 main aspects of their approach divided into theoretical and practical features.

*The CBT Distinctive Features Series* will be essential reading for psychotherapists, counsellors, and psychologists of all orientations who want to learn more about the range of new and developing cognitive-behavioural approaches.

**Titles in the series:**

*Acceptance and Commitment Therapy* by Paul Flaxman and J.T. Blackledge

*Beck's Cognitive Therapy* by Frank Wills

*Behavioral Activation* by Jonathan Kanter, Andrew Busch and Laura Rusch

*Compassion Focused Therapy* by Paul Gilbert

*Constructivist Psychotherapy* by Robert A. Neimeyer

*Dialectical Behaviour Therapy* by Michaela Swales and Heidi Heard

*Metacognitive Therapy* by Peter Fisher and Adrian Wells

*Mindfulness-Based Cognitive Therapy* by Rebecca Crane

*Rational Emotive Behaviour Therapy* by Windy Dryden

*Schema Therapy* by Eshkol Rafaeli, David P. Bernstein and Jeffrey Young

For further information about this series please visit www.routledgementalhealth.com/cbt-distinctive-features

# Metacognitive Therapy

## Distinctive Features

**Peter Fisher and Adrian Wells**

Routledge
Taylor & Francis Group

LONDON AND NEW YORK

First published 2009 by Routledge
27 Church Road, Hove, East Sussex BN3 2FA

Simultaneously published in the USA and Canada
by Routledge
270 Madison Avenue, New York NY 10016

Routledge is an imprint of the Taylor & Francis Group,
an Informa business

Reprinted 2010 (four times)

Typeset in Times by Garfield Morgan,
Swansea, West Glamorgan
Printed and bound in Great Britain by
TJ International Ltd, Padstow, Cornwall
Cover design by Sandra Heath

British Library Cataloguing in Publication Data
A catalogue record for this book is available from the British Library

Library of Congress Cataloging in Publication Data
Fisher, Peter, 1968-
   Metacognitive therapy : distinctive features / Peter Fisher and
Adrian Wells.
       p. ; cm.
   Includes bibliographical references and index.
   ISBN 978-0-415-43498-0 (hbk.) – ISBN 978-0-415-43499-7 (pbk.) 1.
Metacognitive therapy. I. Wells, Adrian. II. Title.
   [DNLM: 1. Cognitive Therapy–methods. 2. Mental Disorders–
therapy. WM 425.5.C6 F535m 2009]
   RC489.M46F57 2009
   616.89'1425–dc22

                                                        2008037541

ISBN: 978-0-415-43498-0 (hbk)
ISBN: 978-0-415-43499-7 (pbk)

# Contents

# Introduction

Metacognitive therapy (MCT) originated with Adrian Wells after he identified a common set of processes in patients suffering from psychological disorder. The approach developed from attempts to explain laboratory findings on biases in attention, and reconcile these with clinical observations of patients who described particular styles of processing as a means of coping. These processes were excessive self-focused attention, attentional bias, worry and rumination.

In the late 1980s and early 1990s, the prevailing view was that attentional bias and worry were automatic processes. It was also the case that mood and anxiety disorders were linked to the content of negative thoughts rather than to specific styles of thinking. In contrast to this explanation, attentional bias and worry were viewed by Wells and colleagues (e.g. Wells & Matthews, 1994) as linked primarily to the person's conscious strategies for appraising and dealing with threat. Furthermore, the content of thoughts was seen as less important than the style and control of thinking in causing psychological disorder. Content does matter in MCT but this is the content of metacognition rather than the content of ordinary cognition.

The integration of laboratory findings with clinical observation culminated in an information processing model of psychological disorder, the Self-Regulatory Executive Function model (S-REF; Wells & Matthews, 1994). The S-REF is the generic basis of disorder-specific metacognitive models and the foundation for MCT.

This book describes the key distinctive theoretical and practical features of MCT and contrasts this approach with cognitive-behavioural therapy. Although both approaches deal with cognition, they provide different accounts of how cognition maintains disorder and they focus on different aspects of thinking. Specifically, MCT asserts that it isn't *what* people think that counts, but *how*.

# Part 1

# THE DISTINCTIVE THEORETICAL FEATURES OF MCT

1

# A focus on metacognition

Metacognition is a term used to refer to a specific category of thinking and cognition. It is essentially cognition applied to cognition. Thinking requires metacognitive factors that monitor and control it. For instance, the process of memorizing a new telephone number depends on knowledge of strategies that can be used to modify memory (e.g. rote rehearsal). It requires the initiation and regulation of the rehearsal strategy, and depends on monitoring when it is time to stop rehearsal. In addition, it requires the subsequent accessing of information that drives retrieval of the number as and when required. In this small example of cognition, the act of memorizing requires multiple aspects of metacognition to make it possible. Beyond this example, metacognition is involved in the cessation, perpetuation and modification of thinking, which encompasses the dysfunctional thinking that maintains psychological disorder.

Traditional cognitive-focused treatments such as cognitive-behaviour therapy (CBT; Beck, 1976) and rational emotive-behaviour therapy (REBT; Ellis, 1962) emphasize the role of cognitive bias and distorted or irrational beliefs rather than the control of thinking. Moreover, these are beliefs outside the metacognitive domain such as beliefs about the world, and the social and physical self. For example, Beck (1976) describes cognitive distortions such as arbitrary inference (jumping to conclusions), catastrophizing, and personalization as cognitive distortions that are evident in negative automatic thoughts. These are different from the thinking styles that are given central prominence in metacognitive therapy (MCT; Wells, 2000). In MCT, maladaptive thinking styles refer to a preponderance of verbal conceptual activity that is difficult to control and occurs

3

in the form of worry and rumination. These styles can be identified independently of their content, as extended forms of brooding and dwelling and analysing information.

In contrast to standard CBT that focuses on a wide range of beliefs about the self and world and says little about metacognitions, metacognitive therapy (MCT) gives metacognitions and metacognitive beliefs a central role in psychological disorder. Unlike CBTs, MCT does not assume that distorted cognitions (i.e. thoughts) and coping behaviours emanate from ordinary beliefs, but specifies that thought patterns are the result of metacognition acting on thinking processes.

Until the advent of metacognitive therapy, research on metacognition was confined largely to the field of developmental psychology and research on human memory. However, Wells and Matthews (1994, 1996) and Wells (2000) developed a general theory of psychopathology that explicitly placed metacognition at centre stage. This approach has led to the development of MCT that aims to change the way individuals experience and control thinking, and the beliefs they hold about cognition. MCT differs from earlier forms of CBT because it does not focus on beliefs and thoughts about the social and physical self, or thoughts and beliefs about others and the environment. Instead, it deals with the way in which people respond to these other cognitions and the mental processes that repeatedly give rise to erroneous and unhelpful views of reality. For example, in cognitive therapy the therapist deals with a patient's cognition about failure by asking, "What is the evidence that you will fail?" but the metacognitive therapist asks, "What is the use in worrying about failure?" The aim in MCT is to modify the thinking processes that support biased failure-oriented processing and the nature of the person's unhelpful reaction to cognitions of this kind.

If we assume that cognition in psychological disorder is biased, as do all cognitive and MCT theories, then it is necessary to identify the source of that bias so that it may be treated. The nature of bias emphasized in CBT, REBT and MCT is different. In the former two approaches it resides in the schemas or irrational beliefs or in the content of negative automatic thoughts. In contrast, in MCT the bias occurs in the style that thinking takes and this is derived from metacognitive knowledge stored as a library of information and plans or programmes that direct processing.

The MCT approach proposes that psychological disorder is linked to a specific style of thinking, involving recurrent, recyclic ideation in the form of worry and rumination and fixating attention on threat. The bias in processing is therefore in how the person thinks rather than in what the person thinks. The content of worry and rumination may show considerable within-individual variation but the process itself remains a constant variable. This process arises from and is controlled by the person's metacognition.

In contrast to this assertion, Beck's schema theory (e.g. 1976) attributes the control of cognition to more general beliefs, which are thought to introduce bias, but this bias is in content rather than in style. Earlier approaches have not attributed a role to metacognition or differentiated between different thinking styles, making MCT distinct in these important respects.

2

# An information processing model of psychological disorder

Metacognitive therapy is grounded in an information processing model of the factors involved in the etiology and maintenance of psychological disorder. The model, called the Self-Regulatory Executive Function (S-REF) model, was originally proposed by Wells and Matthews (1994) and has been subsequently elaborated (Wells, 2000, 2009). As the name of the model implies, it accounts for psychological disorders in terms of predominantly top-down or conscious processes and self-regulatory strategies. According to the model, the person's style of thinking or coping with thoughts, emotions and stress backfire, and lead to an intensification and maintenance of emotional distress. The model draws on distinctions in cognitive psychology between levels of control of attention. It proposes that psychological disturbance is principally linked to biases in the selection and execution of controlled processes for appraising and coping with thoughts, threats and emotions. An individual's strategy for thinking and self-regulation in response to threat and challenges can prolong emotional suffering or lead to more transient emotional reactions. Psychological disorder develops when the person's style of thinking and coping inadvertently leads to persistence and strengthening of emotional responses. This occurs principally as a result of *extended thinking* which prolongs emotion. A certain pattern of thinking, called the cognitive attentional syndrome (CAS), is identified as a causal factor in extending negative thinking in psychological disorder.

Unlike cognitive-behavioural theory, MCT theory does not link psychological problems to automatic processing biases or the content of schemas but attributes them to the individual's conscious strategies. For example, attentional bias, like that observed in the emotional Stroop task, is not attributed to activation of schemas or automatic processing but is attributed to the person's choice of strategy. In psychological disorder, patients have a strategy of maintaining attention on sources of threat and engaging in worry-based processing as a means of coping. Filtering tasks such as the Stroop are thought to be sensitive to these aspects of processing strategy (Wells & Matthews, 1994).

The S-REF model is based on three basic levels of cognition: a level of reflexive and automatic processes that run with minimal or no conscious involvement. These processes may generate intrusions into consciousness that capture attention. The next level is an online form of processing, which is conscious and capacity-limited, responsible for regulating and implementing appraisal and action. The final level is stored knowledge in long-term memory. The immediate activities of the online processing require access to stored knowledge in order to run. Online processing is guided by knowledge or beliefs that are metacognitive in nature. Among these levels, two domains of cognition are important: the metacognitive and cognitive domains. This overall structure or "architecture" of cognition is different from that in traditional CBT, as it maps onto levels of control of cognition and differentiates between the content of thoughts and the regulation of thinking, which is not a distinction made in traditional approaches.

In CBT, there are no levels of attention with a dynamic interaction between them; instead, there are components of cognition such as the distinction made between negative automatic thoughts and beliefs or schemas. A schema in CBT is a memory structure that is synonymous with ideas such as "I'm worthless" or "I'm losing my mind", which are beliefs thought to be behind psychological disorder. It is not clear how these beliefs actually control thinking. In MCT, beliefs like these can be viewed as outputs of processing and what matters is the style of thinking and metacognition that extends and repeatedly generates these concepts.

Traditional CBT does not make a distinction between automatic or controlled processing or consider which factors might lead to the types of appraisal or self-regulatory responses seen in mental disorders. For instance, it assumes that disorder is linked to negative automatic thoughts, which are rapid short-hand negative appraisals such as "I'm dying" or "I'm a failure". However, metacognitive theory views these types of appraisal as relatively normal and transient occurrences; they are not the source of disorder. Instead, S-REF theory asserts that it is the way an individual responds to such thoughts that determines whether or not psychological disorder develops. Similarly, a belief or schema is not thought to be stored in long-term memory but is simply considered to be another example of a thought that is reliably triggered and which the person might subsequently appraise as valid. So beliefs in metacognitive theory are instances of currently activated thoughts and appraisals of their validity; beliefs are a product of online processing. The content of thoughts may be erroneous but the person acts as if a thought is a direct read-out of reality because of the mode of processing in which it occurs. Thus, in MCT it is not merely the content of belief or thoughts that is important but the way an individual responds to that thought and the individual's processing mode. We will return to the concept of modes later (Point 5).

To illustrate the idea that the content of thoughts or beliefs may not be especially important in disorder, we can consider two individuals who have the same experience and the same negative automatic thought or belief. Let's assume they are students who fail an examination and this activates the thought or belief: "I'm a failure." One student becomes depressed and the other experiences only short-term disappointment. How can this be when they have the same experiences and negative automatic thought? Traditional CBT cannot answer this question because it places all its emphasis on the content of negative automatic thoughts and beliefs.

MCT offers an answer to this conundrum. It states that it is not the thought itself but the individual's reaction to that thought (or reaction to a belief) that determines its emotional and longer-term consequences for wellbeing. Some individuals are more resilient than others, which is probably because they are more flexible in their responses to negative thoughts and emotions. They maintain flexible control over their responses and do not become locked into patterns of sustained processing of negative information that prolongs emotional distress. Such flexibility includes the capacity to modulate activity in low-level processing structures such as the amygdala, as well as disrupt and switch out of sustained or extended conceptual processing.

In the S-REF model, a particular style of sustained and inflexible responding to thoughts, emotion and threats is responsible for prolonging and intensifying suffering; this style is called the Cognitive Attentional Syndrome (CAS).

3

# The cognitive attentional syndrome (CAS)

According to S-REF theory and MCT, a particular style of thinking and ways of coping with negative ideas and threat are a fundamental feature of all psychological disorders. This style, called the CAS, consists of persistent thinking in the form of worry and rumination, focusing attention on sources of threat, and coping behaviours that backfire because they impair effective self-regulation of thoughts and emotions and learning of corrective information. If we return to the example of the students who failed, introduced in Point 2, the one who became depressed engaged in brooding on the reasons for being a failure, why it had happened this time and why it had happened in the past and what this meant about his ability. This form of conceptual analysis is rumination and it prolongs and intensifies negative ideas and emotions. It focuses on analysing why things happened and what this means; however, in the misguided pursuit of understanding, it rarely generates useful solutions or exerts more adaptive control over emotional processing. The more adaptive solution is represented by the response of the student who did not become depressed. This individual engaged in a short period of brooding but then decided that the best thing to do was focus on how he could improve his performance the next time around. In effect, this student exercised control over his rumination and activated a different strategy in response to thoughts/beliefs about being a failure.

Rumination is predominantly past-focused. In contrast, a similar conceptual process that is also part of the CAS, worry, is mainly future-oriented. A short-hand means of distinguishing each process is that rumination seeks answers to "why"

**11**

questions, whereas worry seeks answers to "what if" questions. Worry is concerned with anticipating threat and generating ways of either coping with it or avoiding it. So a person may have a quick negative thought: "What if I fail the interview?" and then engage in sustained worry in response to this thought. Worrying is a chain of thoughts in which the person contemplates a range of threatening events and ways to deal with them. So a worry sequence may proceed something like this: "What if I fail the interview . . . I'd better be prepared . . . but what if I haven't prepared the right thing . . . what should I prepare . . . I know, I'll look at the job description . . . but what if they ask about my weaknesses . . . should I tell them about leaving my last job . . . what if they think I'm not good enough . . . what should I tell them . . . what if I say the wrong thing . . . what if I get too nervous . . .?"

The problem with worry as a response to negative ideas or feelings is that it generates a range of threats and increases the sense of danger, leading to anxiety or maintaining an existing anxiety response. Worry and rumination may have other effects on lower levels of processing. In particular, in the metacognitive model of post-traumatic stress disorder (PTSD) (Wells, 2000; Wells & Sembi, 2004a), worry and rumination are thought to disrupt normal in-built recovery processes following trauma, leading to a perpetuation of a sense of threat and to symptoms of PTSD. This is partly because the individual fails to execute the appropriate top-down control over activity in emotion-processing networks in the brain. Instead, resources needed for control are diverted to emotion-laden processes of worry and rumination, which sensitize or sustain activity in emotional networks.

In addition to worry and rumination, the CAS also consists of an attentional strategy of threat monitoring. This refers to fixating attention on threatening stimuli. Often in psychological disorder these are internal events such as thoughts, bodily sensations or emotions. For instance, the obsessional patient monitors for occurrences of certain forbidden or dangerous thoughts; the person with contamination fears monitors for "suspicious-looking" stains on the floor; the person with health anxiety checks his body for signs of disease; and the person with social phobia monitors how they think they appear to others. In each case, threat monitoring increases access to negative information and maintains the sense of threat.

Another important aspect of the CAS is unhelpful coping behaviours, such as avoidance of feared situations, reassurance seeking, trying to control thoughts, using alcohol or drugs, neutralizing behaviours and self-punishment. These strategies backfire for a range of reasons, including the negative effect they have on others, the fact that they prevent exposure to information that can correct erroneous ideas, and that some of them interrupt normal cognitive and biological processes.

The identification of a specific style of thinking (the CAS) sets MCT apart from other forms of CBT because it is more concerned with processes than with content of thought. In MCT, it is not necessary to challenge the content of a thought such as "I'm a failure" but, rather, to help the individual develop an alternative relationship to that thought whilst abandoning the CAS.

A further distinctive feature of MCT is the level of detail used in differentiating between types of human cognition contributing to disorder. It sees negative automatic thoughts as triggers for more sustained worry or rumination and these latter processes are the more proximal cause of disorder. This distinction between varieties of thought is not made in CBT or REBT approaches. Moreover, psychological disorder in MCT is linked to sustained processing and not to the brief instances of thoughts – "automatic thoughts" – that can occur on the periphery of consciousness.

Further important distinctive theoretical features of MCT will emerge in Point 4, as we consider the underlying psychological factors that give rise to the CAS.

4

# Metacognitive beliefs

MCT gives prominence to metacognitive beliefs in the develop-ment and maintenance of psychological suffering. It holds that a relatively small and specific range of beliefs can explain almost all pathology. This is different from CBT and REBT, in which there are many types of schemas or irrational beliefs. In schema theory, a new schema is formulated whenever it is needed to fit the patient's presenting problem.

In MCT, positive and negative metacognitive beliefs are important (modification of these beliefs is discussed in Points 21 and 22). Other approaches do not formulate metacognitive beliefs and do not classify the ones that are important. Positive beliefs concern the advantages of worrying, ruminating, threat monitoring and controlling of cognition. An example of a positive metacognitive belief is: "Worrying about the future means I'll always be prepared." In addition to these positive meta-beliefs, negative meta-beliefs are also given prominence. These beliefs concern the uncontrollability of thoughts and their importance or dangerous consequences. An example of a negative metacognition is: "Thinking about X will make me lose my mind; I have no control over my worrying."

These metacognitive beliefs give rise to the CAS because they support persistent worry-based or ruminative thinking styles and threat monitoring. They also give rise to unhelpful patterns of cognitive self-regulation, such as attempts to suppress certain thoughts, but also to failure to disengage mental processes, such as worry or rumination, that can be controlled (e.g. "If you believe worry is uncontrollable, do you try to stop it?").

Different metacognitive beliefs within the domains already specified are thought to be prominent in specific disorders. In generalized anxiety disorder (GAD), the metacognitive model (Wells, 1995) gives particular importance to negative beliefs about the uncontrollability of worry and the danger of worrying for physical and psychosocial functioning. Despite the fact that patients have such negative metacognitive beliefs they also hold the more normal belief that worrying is advantageous for anticipating threat and planning coping strategies. MCT is unique in its emphasis on negative metacognitive beliefs about worry and the role of negative appraisal of worry as uncontrollable and dangerous in the pathogenesis and treatment of GAD.

In the metacognitive model of obsessive-compulsive disorder (OCD) (Wells, 1997, 2000), metacognitive beliefs concern the importance, meaning and danger of having intrusive thoughts. These beliefs are in the domains of thought–action fusion (TAF: "Thinking of jumping off the bridge will make me do it"), thought–event fusion (TEF: "Thinking that my partner will have an accident will make it more likely to happen"), and thought–object fusion (TOF: "My bad thoughts can contaminate my best possessions and ruin them"). In addition to fusion-related beliefs about thoughts, in this model, beliefs about the need to react to thoughts in special ways and perform rituals are also important. MCT is unique in identifying and focusing specifically on a range of fusion-related beliefs and in identifying beliefs about rituals.

Concepts that appear similar to metacognitive beliefs also appear in other specific cognitive theories of OCD, but these are superficial rather than a substantive point of overlap. For example, Salkovskis (1985) presents a cognitive model of OCD in which individuals interpret intrusive thoughts as a sign that they are responsible for causing or preventing harm. However, responsibility is a very broad concept that does not specifically define or describe the nature of metacognitions underlying such appraisals. Rachman (1997) introduced a refinement of the responsibility concept and discussed the role of cognitive distortions in the form of Thought–Action Fusion (TAF). This occurs in two forms: probability and morality TAF. Probability refers to the idea that having a thought will increase the likelihood of an event, while morality refers to the idea that having a thought is morally equivalent to performing an unwanted act. These concepts refer to metacognitive phenomena but view them as distortions. In metacognitive theory of OCD, which retains the fusion nomenclature, fusion is conceptualized as a series of beliefs (TEF, TAF and TOF) as outlined above and no role is given to the morality dimension. Thus, it can be seen that there is some overlap between Rachman's concept of fusion and the beliefs of metacognitive theory but this is minor, while there is little or no overlap with the concept of inflated responsibility in OCD theory.

The metacognitive model of PTSD (Wells, 2000; Wells & Sembi, 2004a) is based on the idea that positive metacognitive beliefs concern the need to engage in repeated thinking about the trauma, worry about future traumas, focus attention on threat and suppress intrusive thoughts (e.g. "I must worry about similar events in the future in order to be prepared"). In addition, there are negative beliefs about the meaning and consequence of symptoms, such as intrusive thoughts and memories (e.g. "If I continue to think in this way, I'll lose my mind"). These metacognitions give rise to persistent recyclic processing of the trauma and increase attention to threat in a way that maintains the individual's sense of danger and anxiety symptoms. Thus, thinking fails to revert automatically to its usual pre-trauma style. No other theories or models implicate metacognitive beliefs in PTSD. Moreover, MCT focuses on modifying the CAS and associated metacognitive beliefs, whilst other CBT approaches focus on modifying the nature of trauma memories.

The metacognitive model of depression (Wells, 2009; Wells & Papageorgiou, 2004) proposes that depression results from the activation of rumination and maladaptive coping behaviours in response to sadness or negative thoughts. Rumination consists of perseverative negative thinking about the causes and meaning of sadness or depression (e.g. Nolen-Hoeksema, 1991; Nolen-Hoeksema et al., 1993). These processes are linked to positive metacognitive beliefs about the advantages of rumination (e.g. "Thinking about why I feel sad will help me to recover") and negative beliefs about the uncontrollability of depressive thoughts and experiences (e.g. "I have no control over my depressive thoughts; they are a sign of disease"). These beliefs lead to a persistence of ruminative thinking styles and the preference of rumination-focused responses to sadness over and above alternative low levels of conceptual activity and increased behaviours. There are sharp contrasts between Beck's schema theory of depression (e.g. Beck et al., 1979) and the MCT approach. The beliefs emphasized in schema theory are in the domains captured by the concept of the negative cognitive triad. They consist of negative beliefs about the self, the world and the future. These beliefs are not a feature of the metacognitive model and are seen as the content or product of rumination. Only MCT gives a fundamental role to beliefs about rumination.

The metacognitive beliefs in other disorders such as social phobia and panic-disorder similarly lead the individual to activate cycles of worry or rumination and to focus attention on threat because of the advantages that this is believed to bestow. However, in each case there is also the belief that these thinking processes are uncontrollable. Each of these beliefs contributes to the persistence of the CAS and to the maintenance and strengthening of distress. For example, the person with social phobia believes that it is helpful to worry about possible mistakes or about creating a favourable impression in the future as a means of ensuring good outcomes. But such worry is often appraised as uncontrollable, and each of these beliefs contributes to a persistence of the activity and to high levels of anxiety.

It follows, from the analysis described above, that major differences exist between the MCT approach to beliefs and CBT theories that are based on schemas or concepts of irrational beliefs. REBT identifies a specific set of beliefs that are primarily in the social domains of acceptance, relationships and personal performance. Schema theory effectively posits an unlimited number of beliefs that seem to best fit the disorder presented. In contrast, MCT implies that all disorders can be linked to a higher level of metacognitive beliefs about thinking and that these fall into positive and negative content categories. The negative category is further reduced to a content of uncontrollability and danger, whilst the positive domain concerns the advantages of worry, rumination and attentional threat-monitoring strategies. These belief domains do not feature in other cognitive-behavioural or "new-wave" therapies. Furthermore, MCT specifies that metacognitive beliefs about uncontrollability and danger of cognition are present in most types of psychological disorder.

So far we have described beliefs as verbal propositions but, unlike CBT or REBT, MCT states that beliefs may not actually be best conceptualized only in this way. They are considered to exist as procedures or plans for processing (Wells & Matthews, 1994). Thus, a cognitive belief such as "I'm worthless" may be the output of a metacognitive plan that controls processing. The plan or programme repeatedly generates this output in certain situations. A metacognitive belief such as, "I must worry in order to avoid problems in the future" is a marker for the programme that supports the process of worrying. Therefore it is necessary to modify the plan itself in therapy and not simply challenge the output or the marker. As a result, MCT incorporates procedures that modify the person's style of processing, such as the focus of attention, style of thinking, and method of coping in problematic situations when the plan is normally activated. In this way, new plans for controlling processing can be developed that increase flexibility in responses and can override the old thinking pattern.

Experiential exercises involving manipulations of attention and awareness, and changing the relationship individuals have with their thoughts provide a means of establishing new plans for reacting to inner events triggered by problematic situations. In other words, tacit metacognitive knowledge, i.e. plans, control processing and are formulated and addressed in treatment. Such treatment is provided not through verbal challenging methods but through experiential strategies of using cognition differently. For example, in the treatment of trauma the therapist asks patients to allow intrusive thoughts to come and go without engaging with them, and in anxiety-provoking situations helps patients to focus attention on benign or safety-related information rather than potential danger.

5

# Object and metacognitive modes

A distinctive theoretical feature of MCT is the idea that cognition can be separated into cognitive and metacognitive systems and that processing can be cognitive or metacognitive in nature. This division raises the possibility that a person can experience thoughts in different modalities. Thoughts can be experienced as external events that are indistinguishable from events that actually occur or they can be experienced as simply events in the mind. In metacognitive therapy, the former mode of experiencing thoughts is called the object mode, whilst the latter is called the metacognitive mode (Wells, 2000). For example, an individual suffering from contamination obsessions repeatedly has the thought; "It's contaminated with faeces" when encountering stains in public places. This person is in object mode and does not differentiate between the thought and the perception of the stain. In metacognitive mode, this person would be aware of the thought and see it as separate from the stain and as an event in the mind. In this way the problem is transformed from one of contamination everywhere to one of giving thoughts too much importance and fusing them with reality.

When an individual experiences a negative thought or belief, such as "I'm worthless", it is typically experienced in object mode; it is taken as a piece of direct data. The person is therefore likely to respond to it by analysing why they are worthless and how they can gain more worth. However, this belief could also be experienced by the person in metacognitive mode. In this mode, the individual steps back from the belief and sees it as a thought in the mind. This shifting of modes is thought to be a valuable resource that increases flexibility in responses to negative ideas that can buffer against the activation of habitual patterns of thinking typified by the CAS. In other forms of CBT, there is objectification of thoughts too, in so much as they are interrogated and reality-tested, but the individual does not directly experience the thought as an object in the mind. This direct experiencing is necessary to strengthen the metacognitive plans that control cognition.

In object mode, thoughts are experienced as direct perceptions and there is no separation between self as observer and the act of thinking itself. Even questioning the validity of a thought, a common practice in CBT, may not counteract this mode of processing. For instance, an individual who thinks, "What if I'm not prepared?" may be led to question the evidence for this appraisal. In so doing, the person imbues the thought with greater objectivity; it is a concept that may or may not be accurate. The individual may not enter a complete metacognitive mode and learn that thoughts are internal events that do not need to be responded to with further thoughts. Instead, they learn that all negative thoughts need to be evaluated for reality; the idea being that, "I cannot trust some thoughts; which ones can I trust?"

6

# Reformulated ABC analysis

The metacognitive model's analysis of psychological disorder is focused "downstream" or "upstream" of that of CBT or REBT. In CBT or REBT, the therapist focuses on negative automatic thoughts or irrational beliefs. In MCT, the therapist focuses on the individual's reactions to thoughts and beliefs or the thinking style that gives rise to beliefs. Reference to the ABC model, on which Ellis' REBT and Beck's CBT are based, provides one way to understand this difference.

In these original examples, "A" refers to an antecedent or activating event that leads to activation of a belief (Ellis) or a negative automatic thought (Beck) designated as "B", which in turn leads to an emotional consequence, "C".

In Wells' MCT, the activating event "A" is specifically re-designated as a cognition (a thought or belief) or emotion which leads to the activation of metacognitive beliefs, "B", and the CAS, which gives rise to emotional consequences, "C". In this schematic, the ordinary negative beliefs or thoughts ("B") are moderated by or caused by "M".

This gives rise to a different formulation of a problem, as illustrated in Figures 1(a) and (b).

What does this mean in terms of treatment? It means that the therapist focuses on beliefs about thoughts rather than beliefs about other types of event. For example, in hypochondriasis the CBT therapist focuses on challenging conviction in thoughts that are misinterpretations of bodily symptoms (e.g. "What's your evidence that you have heart disease?"). However, in MCT the therapist questions the patient about the need to continuously appraise symptoms in this way (e.g. "What's the point in repeatedly worrying that you have heart disease?").

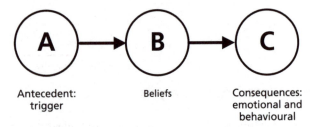

**Figure 1a** ABC analysis
Source: Wells (2009, p. 17). Copyright 2009 by Guilford Press. Reprinted by permission.

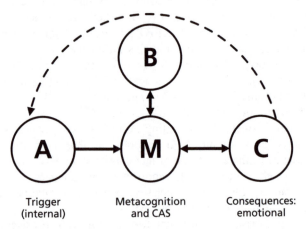

**Figure 1b** AMC analysis
Source: Wells (2009, p. 18). Copyright 2009 by Guilford Press. Reprinted by permission.

The MCT question reveals metacognitive beliefs about uncontrollability of thoughts and positive beliefs about the need to misinterpret symptoms and worry about health in order to remain safe. The MCT therapist challenges these metacognitions and explores alternative ways of relating to symptoms that do not necessitate worry or misinterpretations.

In the AMC analysis, metacognitions may repeatedly generate other instances of negative thoughts or beliefs as, for instance, an output of worry or rumination sequences. So a trigger may be an intrusive mental event, which primes metacognitions that guide processing in a way that generates the more conscious negative appraisals that would normally be classed as thoughts or beliefs.

7

# Detached mindfulness

Because the CAS links disorder to styles of responding to thoughts and beliefs, an aim of treatment is to develop alternative styles of responding to these inner events. As we have seen, the CAS refers to a state of processing consisting of worry, rumination, threat monitoring, suppression and other maladaptive coping behaviours. Wells and Matthews (1994) introduced the term "detached mindfulness" (DM) to refer specifically to an alternative state of processing that is the antithesis of the CAS and also aims to shift the patient from object-mode to metacognitive mode of processing.

As the name suggests, detached mindfulness comprises two features: mindfulness and detachment. Mindfulness simply refers to being aware of the occurrence of a thought or belief; this is essentially developing and activating meta-awareness. The second component is detachment. This refers to two factors: (a) the suspension of any conceptual or coping activity in response to the thought, and (b) the separation of sense of self from the thought. A wide range of techniques and strategies has been developed to help individuals acquire the metacognitive skills necessary to deploy the state of DM (e.g. Wells, 2005). However, DM is not intended to be a symptom management, avoidance or coping strategy; it is intended to increase the array of flexible responses to thoughts, beliefs and feelings when they are activated.

The range of strategies developed includes metacognitive guidance, the free-association task, the tiger task and the use of metaphors in treatment (see Point 25 for a discussion of these strategies).

Detached mindfulness has no parallel with techniques used in earlier forms of CBT. However, mindfulness meditation techniques have recently been used as strategies for treating relapse prevention in mindfulness based cognitive therapy for depression (e.g. Teasdale et al., 2000).

DM may overlap a little with the concept and practice of mindfulness meditation. There are minor similarities in that both are intended to reduce or suspend evaluative types of processing. However, they differ substantially because DM is specifically aimed at suspending continued conceptual processing of thoughts, whereas meditation involves a more general "acceptance" of all events. Mindful meditation is also linked to adopting an inquisitive stance in relation to events, but it is difficult to reconcile the idea of non-judgemental processing with acceptance and inquisitiveness that rely on high-level interpretative processes. Meditation is practised over many weeks or years, but DM is applied to specific instances of thoughts and can be developed in minutes. Mindfulness meditation often involves using focusing of attention on internal anchors such as the breath, but DM does not require this type of body-focused attention. Moreover, such self-attention is eschewed because of the risk of its contributing to self-focused processing configurations that are part of the CAS. Meditation is not specifically designed to modify pathological mechanisms and processes, as is the case with DM.

Detached mindfulness in MCT was developed specifically to produce cognitive and metacognitive effects considered helpful on the basis of metacognitive theory. In contrast, mindfulness meditation pre-dates any theory of psychological disorder and was subsequently embraced by theorists wishing to reduce depressive rumination. Thus, DM is developed from a theory of rumination and worry, whereas mindfulness meditation is based on Buddhist practices.

Whilst DM is a component of MCT, it is not necessary or sufficient. It is used as a technique that helps patients develop an alternative relationship with cognition without triggering the

CAS and with a view to enhancing metacognitive control. The technique is specific to MCT and does not feature in other forms of CBT, which prefer to challenge thoughts rather than disengage further processing from them.

8

# Executive control and attentional flexibility

In metacognitive theory, psychological disorder is linked to a loss of cognitive resources and attentional flexibility. This is a problem because psychological change and the control of cognition require processing resources, yet these are constrained by the CAS. Loss of resources and executive control means that individuals have deficiencies in the top-down control or suppression of activity in lower-level and more reflexive emotion processing networks in the brain (i.e. amygdala). In addition, focusing attention on threat limits the person's access to information that can correct faulty ideas in feared situations. It follows that it would be beneficial in treatment to develop techniques that recover resources, increase flexible (executive) control over processing and enhance the flow of corrective information into processing. With this goal in mind, techniques such as Attention Training (Wells, 1990; see Point 24) and Situational Attentional Refocusing (Wells & Papageorgiou, 1998; see Point 26) have been developed as part of MCT.

Attention Training Technique (ATT) consists of external attentional focusing on multiple auditory stimuli and has selective attention, attention switching and divided attention components. It is practised during discrete practice sessions rather than applied as a coping technique. Empirical evidence supports the ameliorative effect of the technique on anxiety and depression (see Wells, 2006, for a review). For example, in experimental studies using case series, ATT has been associated with improvements in symptoms in panic disorder (Wells et al., 1997), hypochondriasis (Papageorgiou & Wells, 1998), and recurrent major depression (Papageorgiou & Wells, 2000). It also appears to be associated with neurobiological changes consisting of reductions in amygdala activity in depressed patients (Siegle et al., 2007). Attention training is often referred to in the "new-wave" CBTs such as Acceptance and Commitment Therapy (ACT; Hayes et al., 1999), but it is not the same thing as ATT (see Point 24).

A different attentional technique used in MCT is Situational Attentional Refocusing (SAR; e.g. Wells & Papageorgiou, 1998). It is used to redirect attention during exposure to threatening or anxiety-provoking situations. The aim is to increase the flow of new and adaptive information into awareness so that the individual is better able to update and modify her erroneous beliefs. For instance, in social phobia individuals turn attention inward onto themselves when entering a feared social situation. This is part of their threat-monitoring and coping strategy, as they fear presenting an unfavourable impression. This attentional style impairs the processing of external information that would be valuable in challenging negative beliefs about other people, such as the belief that everyone is staring at them. In order to modify dysfunctional beliefs, it is necessary to modify the direction of attention during exposure so that it is focused on other people in the environment. Thus, the use of exposure in metacognitive therapy does not depend on repeated or prolonged exposures but depends on controlling cognition during exposure to maximize the efficiency of new learning.

SAR is also applied in MCT for trauma, where the individual's attentional style changes following a traumatic event. Threat monitoring after trauma often consists of focusing on potential sources of danger in the environment, which increases the perception of current danger and maintains anxiety. In order for cognition to return to its usual state of processing, the therapist works with the patient to identify and modify the focus of attention using techniques such as prescribing the detection of neutral stimuli and safety signals in the environment.

9

# Levels of control

Self-Regulatory Executive Function (S-REF) metacognitive theory differs from the theories of Beck and Ellis and most other cognitive approaches to psychopathology in being grounded in information processing theory. It has a cognitive architecture, meaning that it has an overall structure that differentiates knowledge or beliefs, online (attentionally demanding) conscious processing and automatic low-level emotional processing, and the nature of relationships between them. This is important because the relationship between these factors is likely to be a source of disorder and may be more important than the content of negative thoughts or social beliefs. Whilst Beck's schema theory uses terms associated with information processing approaches, such as schema and attention bias, it really focuses on cognitive content rather than explaining in detail how information is transmitted, the form it takes, how it passes through levels from stimulus to response and how levels of cognition are connected. This level of explanation is required for true information processing accounts and is described to a greater degree in the S-REF model.

The S-REF represents cognition within a three-level architecture: (1) low-level automatic processing networks that process information reflexively and outside awareness and incorporate primitive emotion-processing networks; (2) a level of conscious strategic processing that requires processing resources, is largely conscious, and is responsible for interpreting and implementing strategies; and (3) a level of stored knowledge that is metacognitive in nature and guides the nature of processing.

Differentiating between levels and describing the interrelationship between them is important because it allows consideration of the roles of automatic highly-learned responses, low-level (sub-cortical) emotional processes, and how they interact with conscious processes in contributing to psychological disorder. The approach therefore has implications for research on neurobiological processes. For instance, it proposes links between strategic processing and activity in emotional-processing circuits and structures in the brain that can be tested and modified. One implication is that the CAS blocks adequate top-down control of emotional processing; thus removing the CAS should provide a means of restoring control and allowing emotional processing to run its normal course and be modulated effectively. This is a basic supposition of MCT for posttraumatic stress disorder.

The distinction between levels and specification of their interrelationship locates disorder predominantly at the level of strategic or conscious processes linked to metacognitive beliefs. Thus, MCT theory differs from early cognitive accounts of bias in emotional disorder (e.g. Williams et al., 1988) by emphasizing the effect of strategic online processes rather than automatic biases in attention. It differs from Beck's (1976) cognitive theory in that it does not equate cognitive biases and distortions with the activity of schemas, but with the style of conscious processing which draws from metacognition. Similarly, it attributes bias effects observed in tasks such as the emotional Stroop test (e.g. Mathews & Macleod, 1985) to strategy-related processes such as maintaining attention on sources of threat (threat monitoring), rather than to automatic processes. This has implications for developing treatments of bias: it means that the therapist should modify the metacognitive beliefs that support threat-monitoring strategies and patients should be instructed in using alternative attentional responses.

The use of ATT and SAR and the focus on modifying metacognitions controlling attention are distinctive features of MCT. When attentional strategies are used in CBT or stress-management treatment approaches, they concentrate on employing distraction from thoughts, emotion or pain experiences as a coping technique. In contrast, attention modification in MCT is designed and delivered with the goal of removing the CAS, strengthening metacognitive control and improving access to new information for updating knowledge.

10

# Types of knowledge

We have already seen how the metacognitive approach differentiates metacognitive knowledge from other knowledge about the self and the world. Another area of contrast with other cognitive theories is the way in which knowledge is represented. CBT and REBT refer to the semantic content of knowledge and express their respective schemas or irrational beliefs in verbal declarative form (e.g. "I'm worthless" and "I must be approved of by virtually everyone in order to be worthwhile"). This is a useful heuristic, but metacognitive theory acknowledges that knowledge is not likely to be represented in this way in the cognitive system, and it may be more useful to think of knowledge as a set of programmes or plans that direct thinking and action (Wells & Matthews, 1994, 1996). In essence, these are metacognitive programmes for guiding processing, and in this sense constitute a proceduralized knowledge base. The marker for these procedures would be declarative statements such as "I must worry in order to avoid harm", but this declarative belief would be closely linked to plans for guiding the activity of the processing system in the implementation of worrying. In this scenario the modification of beliefs should not only include verbal challenging of the level of conviction in metacognitions but also provide individuals with alternative plans for processing.

For example, the prevention of relapse in anxiety and depression would not only focus on checking for and modifying residual levels of conviction in declarative beliefs, as would be the case in standard CBT, but would also involve training patients to implement new ways of thinking and coping in response to negative thoughts, beliefs and emotions. However, these are not just any type of new response. It is not an issue of generic training in relaxation or social skills, for instance, but is specific training in responses that are opposite to the CAS and any new strategy learned must not be used to avoid or prevent erroneous threat. By shaping and practising new responses, the individual develops the knowledge base or programme to support these new responses in the future.

A distinctive feature of MCT, therefore, is the incorporation of a training component that helps patients strengthen new plans for regulating cognition and action. This typically constitutes part of relapse prevention and distinguishes MCT from other treatment approaches that train anxiety reduction, social interaction, assertiveness or other types of skill.

**11**

# Processes and strategies beyond cognitive content

As we have seen, a key difference between MCT and the approaches of CBT, behaviour therapy and REBT is that it does not focus on the content of thoughts and beliefs. The only exception is reserved for focusing on the content of meta-cognitive beliefs. In CBT, the therapist is concerned with the content of negative automatic thoughts and invites the patient to reality test this content. Cognitive distortions or thinking errors are identified in thoughts and beliefs but this is an extension of examining content. This emphasis on content stands in contrast to the predominant focus of MCT, which is on thinking style or cognitive processes.

In MCT, disorder is viewed as a function not of cognitive content but of processes such as perseverative thinking, attentional focus, and internal control strategies that are counter-productive. Perseverative processes are patterns of recyclic conceptual activity that most commonly take the form of worry or rumination. These processes can have virtually any content and it is necessary in MCT to arrest these processes and restore flexible control over thinking. However, MCT is not about suppressing thought content; it is about interrupting a particular process and learning to relate to thoughts without the need to engage in sustained processing or goal-directed coping.

The metacognitive approach views attention as a central process in pathology. The strategy of threat monitoring is an important feature of the CAS. This strategy is not seen as an automatic function of the person's general beliefs (e.g. "I'm vulnerable"), as in schema-based cognitive therapy, but is viewed as linked to metacognitive beliefs that control attention.

As described in Point 10, the modification of attention through discrete exercises and the situational deployment of new attention strategies in stressful situations is a distinctive feature of MCT. The aim is modification of metacognitions that control attention in the service of strengthening executive control and improving access to new information that can modify knowledge.

In the "pure" version of MCT theory, cognitive content is viewed as the material used by processes and modified by processes. It is the processes that are seen as the core elements of pathology, but these draw on metacognitive content for guidance rather than on any other content of cognition. The range of processes implicated in MCT theory is wider than in schema theory. Furthermore, the link between processes and the content of the person's knowledge is made explicit. In schema theory, processes or "biases" are largely a feature of content rather than separate factors of cognitive style, as is the case in MCT.

# 12

# View of self-awareness

The S-REF model views self-awareness as a complex multi-faceted variable. This sets the approach aside from most other theories and treatments of psychopathology. Often self-awareness is equated with positive mental health outcomes and is a factor reinforced in treatment. The metacognitive approach does not correspond with this view of self-awareness.

First, it views self-focused attention (a component of self-awareness) as a generic marker for activation of the CAS, particularly when self-attention is chronic and inflexible. Second, it views a particular type of self-awareness specifically involving awareness of thoughts as most useful in treatment. However, high degrees of attention given to one's body and public and private self-concept are thought to be deleterious. This is a marker for excessive preoccupation and self-analysis that is a feature of the CAS.

The MCT therapist is cognisant that even awareness of thoughts is not free of potential toxic effects. This awareness may reflect "threat monitoring", as in cases of OCD or PTSD, where individuals fear the occurrences of particular types of thought and monitor them as a means of preventing harm.

Unlike most other psychotherapeutic approaches, MCT signals the necessity to delineate further the nature of awareness of thoughts that is conducive to positive health outcomes. It suggests that the type of awareness that is beneficial is specifically not linked to goal-directed harm avoidance. It is awareness of thoughts or beliefs as passing events in the mind that do not require any response. Adaptive self-awareness is flexible and not directed at coping but allows attention to be freely allocated to observing thoughts without further conceptual processing.

It is recognized that self-awareness can be beneficial when it is flexible, controllable and applied appropriately in a way that does not compromise self-regulation, belief change and performance. Most therapy approaches equate self-awareness to positive health outcomes without defining the kind of self-awareness that is and is not beneficial.

# 13

# Varieties of change

As the foregoing discussion has begun to elucidate, metacognitive therapy opens up a range of new possibilities for therapeutic change that do not figure in traditional CBT. Unlike the focus of traditional treatment on reality-testing the content of negative thoughts and beliefs about the self and the world, MCT focuses on modifying cognitive processes. These are not the processes buried in the content of thoughts (e.g. arbitrary, inference, catastrophizing) as in Beck's CBT, but are the styles of worry, rumination and threat monitoring. MCT aims to suspend these processes, not to test their content against the facts.

The main point at which challenging content enters MCT is when the therapist works on underlying metacognitive beliefs about thoughts – a level of working that is not a feature of earlier CBTs. Treatment uses verbal reattribution methods and behavioural experiments to challenge positive and negative metacognitive beliefs.

Because MCT is based on a distinction between metacognitive and cognitive levels of processing, and the two systems supporting them, it asserts that there are two ways of relating to thoughts and beliefs. Previously, in Point 5, we saw that these are labelled the modes. This distinction gives rise to a type of change that directly alters the individual's experience of his own mental events. It is useful to change the way a person experiences and relates to his thoughts and beliefs. Specifically, it suggests these can be experienced as objects in the mind that are moved outside the sense of the observing self, as would be the goal in detached mindfulness (see Point 7).

Finally, an important variety of change involves the strengthening of control and flexibility of cognition. This does not mean improving the ability to avoid unwanted thoughts. Rather, this means improving control of attention, which acts as a general-purpose resource for prioritizing cognition and action under stressful conditions and attenuating unwanted activity in lower-level processing networks. When a person can control attention they can choose to shape the version of reality inhabited. Attention is the basis of consciousness and of learning about the self and the world.

In summary, metacognitive theory presents a range of targets for change that distinguish the approach from other treatments. It implies that it is possible and beneficial to change: (1) thinking style, (2) content of metacognitions, (3) modes and the nature of experiential awareness of cognition, and (4) strength of executive (attentional) control.

14

## Disorder-specific models

So far we have discussed generic features of the metacognitive model and universal aspects of treatment. However, disorder-specific models have been developed and evaluated that are based on the generic S-REF model. The disorder-specific models are aimed at capturing the content of metacognitions and the nature of processes that are more specific to a particular disorder (see Wells, 2000, 2009). For instance, in generalized anxiety disorder metacognitive beliefs concern positive beliefs about the usefulness of worry whilst negative beliefs concern the uncontrollability and danger of worrying. Both types of belief exist but it is the negative metacognitive beliefs that are the more proximal cause of GAD. In obsessive-compulsive disorder, the metacognitions concern the themes of thought–event fusion (TEF), thought–action fusion (TAF) and thought–object fusion (TOF). In TEF, thoughts are believed to have the power to increase the probability of events (e.g. "Thinking about accidents will make them happen"). In TAF, thoughts are believed to increase the likelihood of committing unwanted acts (e.g. "Thinking of stabbing someone will make me do it"). In TOF, the belief is that thoughts and feelings can be transferred into objects or contaminate or spoil them in some way (e.g. "If I have impure thoughts whilst reading, my thoughts will pass into my books and I won't be able to study in the future").

In depression, metacognitive beliefs focus around positive beliefs about rumination as a means of coping with sadness, and negative beliefs about the uncontrollability and causes of depressive thoughts and feelings. Post-traumatic stress disorder (PTSD) is linked to positive beliefs about worrying as a means of anticipating and avoiding future danger, positive beliefs about the benefits of analysing the traumatic event to reach understanding or apportion blame, and negative beliefs about the meaning and consequences of experiencing intrusive thoughts and recollections of the event.

Two models will now be described in more detail to illustrate the processes and specific metacognitions involved in depression and PTSD. Each of these models and the others alluded to in this section form the basis of generating personal case formulations that are shared with patients as the basis of conducting treatment. MCT proceeds on an individual case formulation basis.

## Metacognitive model of depression

The metacognitive model of depression (Wells, 2009) is depicted in Figure 2. The person with depression responds to negative thoughts and feelings of sadness with activation of positive metacognitive beliefs about the need to ruminate as a means of dealing with sadness and negative thoughts/beliefs. It is typically believed that rumination will lead to a greater understanding and the discovery of solutions to feelings of sadness or thoughts of personal failure or defectiveness.

Rumination consists of chains of thoughts in which the person asks questions such as, "why, what does it mean, if only, why me, will it ever end . . .?" and so on. This process rarely produces answers but focuses the individual more intensely on feelings and memories of failure or negative events and this maintains sadness. At some point in this process the depressed person develops and subsequently activates negative beliefs about depressive thoughts and symptoms. These involve beliefs about the uncontrollability of thoughts and feelings (e.g. "I have no control over my thinking; depression is an illness in my brain beyond my control"). These beliefs lead to further negative thoughts, such as thoughts about hopelessness and behaviours such as social withdrawal, which maintain depression

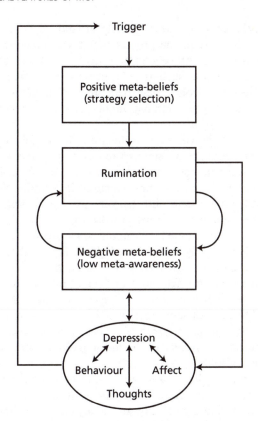

**Figure 2** Metacognitive model of depression

Source: Wells (2009, p. 199). Copyright 2009 by Guilford Press. Reprinted by permission.

and rumination. Another process also contributes to depression. With repeated rumination and depression the person begins to lose awareness of the activity of ruminating. This reduced meta-awareness interferes with the ability to identify and interrupt ruminative responses so that they persist in their cycle of depression unchecked. Furthermore, because the person believes rumination is helpful and may lead to an answer to depression, the process is not spontaneously recognized as the toxic process that it really is. There are other changes in behaviour such as reduced activity levels and coping through use of alcohol that backfire and increase negative thoughts that trigger rumination or provide more time and space for rumination.

A case example will serve to illustrate the model. A 31-year-old woman presented to services reporting multiple depressive episodes over the last eight years. Her current episode of depression had lasted for approximately 18 months. She could not identify any specific life triggers for her depression, but she had been unable to return to work for the past 11 months. The therapist questioned her about how she used her time during a typical day and selected yesterday as the reference point. The patient explained how she carried on with some daily chores but she felt tired and unmotivated most of the time and on some days found it easier to remain in bed. She described feelings of sadness on waking in the morning, and of thinking "It will never improve". These feelings and thoughts are identified as a trigger in the metacognitive model and case conceptualization.

The therapist then asked about the type of thoughts the patient had in response to this trigger and discovered that she spent all morning ruminating and analysing why she felt this way and trying to work out why she was "different". The patient described how this process of rumination occurred about 80 per cent of the time. Asking about the advantages of engaging in this type of thinking activity as a means of exploring positive metacognitive beliefs, the therapist discovered that the patient believed that rumination helped because it acted as a form of punishment that might cause her to become angry and break out of depression. Paradoxically, however, the patient also believed that she had limited control over both her thinking and her emotions and did not see that the process of rumination was a central factor in maintaining her suffering.

In this case example, we can see each of the important aspects of the metacognitive model: there are positive and negative metacognitive beliefs about thinking; the CAS is evident as rumination; and unhelpful coping is apparent in the form of self-punishment, anger and, on some days, remaining in bed.

Treatment consisted of sharing the case formulation, introducing strategies that enabled her to disengage from negative thoughts and feelings and postpone and eventually ban rumination. Treatment challenged metacognitive beliefs, and helped her learn new ways of responding to sadness and negative thoughts in the future.

There are very few similarities between this approach to depression and cognitive-behavioural approaches. Traditional CBT would formulate the problem in terms of the content of negative automatic thoughts and focus on challenging the validity of thoughts centring on the "cognitive triad" (negative thoughts about self, the world and the future). In contrast, MCT does not concern itself with the content of such thoughts and does not reality-test them. It views these thoughts as the trigger for rumination or as an output of rumination and it focuses on changing the process of continued thinking rather than any specific content of thinking. Both approaches might use activity scheduling, but in CBT the goal would be to increase mastery and pleasure, whilst in MCT this would be to counteract inactivity, which is seen as a maladaptive coping behaviour that provides time for rumination. MCT would challenge beliefs about rumination and depression, but CBT would challenge general schemas (beliefs) about the world, the future or the self (e.g. "I'm worthless"). Another important difference is that MCT would utilize specific techniques that are not a part of CBT, such as attention training, detached mindfulness, and metacognitively-focused behavioural experiments that change the way the person relates to thoughts and feelings. In some respects, CBT activities such as keeping thought diaries, interrogating the reality of negative thoughts and identifying the thinking errors they contain would be seen by the MCT practitioner as engaging in excessive thinking processes that are not far enough removed from the CAS.

### Metacognitive model of post-traumatic stress disorder

Post-traumatic stress disorder (PTSD) is the persistence of particular clusters of symptoms (arousal, avoidance, re-experiencing) for longer than one month following exposure to a stressful event. In most instances symptoms subside within this time but in a significant minority of cases they persist. The metacognitive model of PTSD (Wells, 2000; Wells & Sembi, 2004) is based on the idea that it is the activation of the CAS that leads to the persistence of symptoms because it interferes with control of emotional processing. The metacognitive model of PTSD is presented in Figure 3. In this model, traumatic events lead to symptoms of increased arousal, intrusive thoughts and startle sensitivity that are part of the person's in-built Reflexive Adaptation Process (RAP). The RAP is a low-level emotional processing function that serves to bias processing and action as a means of facilitating the acquisition of new routines for cognition and action in the future. Normally, symptoms subside as the RAP runs its course and the individual uses flexible executive control over it.

However, activation of the CAS inhibits flexible control over the RAP and inadvertently fuels the processing of threat and the running of the continued anxiety programme. In particular, worry about threats in the future maintains the sense of danger and anxiety, and rumination about the trauma maintains preoccupation with trauma memory. Strategies such as threat monitoring (e.g. hypervigilance for people who resemble an attacker) increase the perception of potential dangers in the environment, which maintains a state of anxiety. Behaviours such as thought suppression (e.g. trying not to think about the trauma) or avoiding reminders of the event prevent the

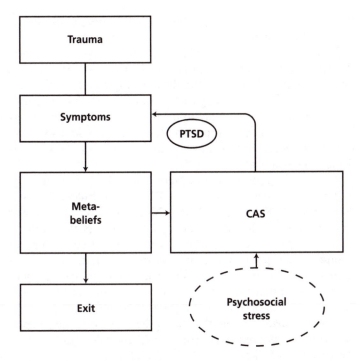

**Figure 3** Metacognitive model of PTSD

Source: Wells (2009, p. 129). Copyright 2009 by Guilford Press. Reprinted by permission.

development of flexible control over thinking, and strategies such as suppression can backfire and increase the salience of thoughts.

The CAS is linked to metacognitive beliefs that include positive beliefs about worry, rumination, threat monitoring and thought control (e.g. "If I worry about being attacked in the future, I'll be prepared; I must keep a look-out for danger in order to prevent accidents"). Negative metacognitive beliefs concern the significance of intrusive thoughts and memories and lead to a sense of continued danger from symptoms themselves (e.g. "Thinking about what happened is out of control; I'm losing my mind").

In summary, as a result of the CAS the individual strengthens the sense of current threat, which maintains anxiety and interacts with the effects of the RAP, giving rise to routines for processing that are configured towards detecting potential dangers and reacting rapidly to them. Threat-related processing is not brought under appropriate flexible control and so cognition does not return to the usual state of processing a relatively benign environment.

The metacognitive model differs markedly from other cognitive and behavioural models of PTSD (e.g. Ehlers & Clark, 2000; Foa & Rothbaum, 1998). Most of these models give special emphasis to disturbances of memory as the cause of PTSD. For instance, it is argued that disorganized memory or failure to incorporate corrective information in memory structures is responsible for symptoms. The metacognitive approach does not hold that either memory disorganization or incomplete memory is important. It suggests that most people have incomplete memories and the hub of the problem is the person's post-trauma thinking style (the CAS) under the influence of metacognitive beliefs.

MCT for PTSD differs extensively from all other cognitive and behavioural treatments. Almost no exposure or imaginal reliving of trauma memories is used in MCT because the mechanism of change is not thought to be change in memory organization, content or habituation to memories. There is no restructuring or rescripting of memories, as would be the case in some types of CBT. There is no challenging of thoughts or beliefs about the trauma or the world. Instead, treatment focuses on developing an idiosyncratic version of the model. Using this formulation, the therapist proceeds to use strategies that reduce worry and rumination. This includes detached mindfulness, worry and rumination postponement experiments, challenging positive beliefs about the need to worry and ruminate, challenging negative beliefs about symptoms, and modifying unhelpful threat-monitoring strategies. These techniques do not appear in other cognitive and behavioural treatments of PTSD.

## 15

## A universal treatment?

There are now many different types of CBT, some of which are linked to well-specified and evidence-based models and others that are not. One of the limitations of CBT is that it is possible to specify any new schema that seems to fit a particular new disorder or presentation. In contrast, MCT is based on a more tightly defined set of variables and beliefs and all disorder can be explained with reference to a small set of pre-specified factors. This means that MCT theory is more parsimonious. It also implies that it may be possible to treat the CAS directly in all disorders, giving rise to a universal or trans-diagnostic treatment approach (Wells, 2009; Wells & Matthews, 1994). It is not clear at this stage whether it would be possible to dispense entirely with the disorder-specific models and these may be retained for optimal treatment effects. However, a universal treatment might be applied to all disorders as a starting point and then disorder-specific modules guided by individual models might then be used as needed. In contrast, the growth of different CBT models has led to an emphasis on the differences between disorders rather than on their similarities and it is unlikely that a universal CBT could emerge from this arena.

# Part 2

# THE DISTINCTIVE PRACTICAL FEATURES OF MCT

# 16

# Conducting therapy at the metacognitive level

The fundamental distinctive feature of metacognitive therapy is the explicit focus on modifying metacognitive beliefs and processes in order to achieve therapeutic change. In other words, MCT concentrates on changing how the patient thinks by altering beliefs about cognition. This is in direct contrast to CBT, which is concerned with the content and product of dysfunctional information processing and therefore the goal is to modify the output of unhelpful thinking (Clark, 2004). The CBT therapists' targets of change include systematic errors, negative automatic thoughts, and core beliefs. In essence, CBT works predominantly at the content or cognitive level, whereas MCT operates at the process or metacognitive level.

Working at the metacognitive level requires the therapist to look beyond the content of ordinary cognition. To accomplish this goal, the MCT therapist must keep in mind the three components of the cognitive attentional syndrome (CAS) – perseverative thinking, maladaptive attentional strategies and unhelpful coping behaviours – and be able to detect and modify each aspect of the CAS during the process of therapy. This gives rise to a very distinctive way of conducting therapy.

To illustrate, imagine you are working with a patient and a sudden affect shift occurs. The CBT therapist might ask, "What just went through your mind?" in order to elicit a negative automatic thought (NAT). The primary goal would be to modify the content of the NAT, or belief in that content, by helping the patient label the cognitive distortion it contains, or by helping the patient to evaluate the evidence and counter-evidence for the NAT with the goal of generating alternative appraisals. Working with the content of thoughts in this way is effectively operating in the object mode, as discussed earlier (Point 5).

The MCT therapist may ask the same initial question, but would make no attempt to modify the content of the NAT because these thoughts are viewed as either a trigger for rumination, or the consequence of a rumination chain. The therapist is therefore interested in the positive metacognitive beliefs that direct the person to select rumination as a coping response and the negative beliefs that make it unlikely the person will interrupt the ruminative process. Modifying these two types of metacognitive belief helps the MCT therapist achieve their therapeutic target of enabling patients to select a non-ruminative response to NATs. In addition, the aim is for patients to realize that such thoughts are simply events in the mind that do not require any form of further conceptual processing.

The difference between working with content in the traditional way and working on the metacognitive level can be further illustrated by comparing CBT and MCT in relation to the following excerpt of ruminative thinking:

I'm alone . . . nobody cares about me . . . why don't my friends or family ring me . . . is this sadness ever going to end? . . . what am I going to do . . . I've felt this way for years . . . I wish I could stop crying . . . nothing works out for me . . . I keep failing . . . why am I so useless?

In this brief rumination sequence, there are a range of negative automatic thoughts, cognitive distortions, possible core beliefs and attributional errors, and therefore the CBT therapist has to decide which cognitive component to target first. The CBT therapist might begin by asking, "What is your evidence for the belief that nobody cares about you? Do you have any counter-evidence against this thought?" As previously discussed, CBT essentially proceeds by reality-testing the content of cognition.

In contrast, the MCT therapist would ask, "Do you think that there are better ways of responding to the thought 'I'm alone'?", with the goals of increasing awareness of the disadvantages of ruminating in response to a negative thought and shifting the patient to a metacognitive mode of processing.

In the above rumination chain, there is a rapid transition from a relatively benign thought, "I'm alone", to being "useless". This is the type of transition that commonly occurs when a CBT therapist conducts a downward arrow. The downward arrow consists of repeatedly questioning what a thought means if it were true and is believed to uncover core beliefs. We suggest that, when a person ruminates, they are effectively conducting their own version of a downward arrow. This is problematic because the person is continually generating negative beliefs about themselves, the world and the future. The MCT therapist would help the patient to identify and label the ruminative process and suspend further analysing, rather than engage in reality-testing the individual negative thoughts. This appears to be a more time-efficient approach to treatment; for example, MCT for depression consists of six–eight one-hour sessions (e.g. Wells et al., in press) compared to the typical 12–16 sessions in traditional CBT (e.g. Dimidjian et al., 2006).

Similarly, when treating patients with obsessive-compulsive disorder (OCD), the MCT therapist focuses on the components of the CAS and metacognitive beliefs about thoughts and rituals, but does not focus on beliefs in other domains (e.g. inflated responsibility). Some minor overlap exists between the metacognitive approach and recent developments in cognitive therapy for OCD. An international working group, the Obsessive-Compulsive Cognitions Working Group (OCCWG, 1997, 2001), began by developing a consensus on the most important belief domains in OCD. These domains are the over-importance of thoughts, the importance of controlling one's thoughts, perfectionism, inflated responsibility, overestimation of threat and intolerance of uncertainty. The first two belief domains are metacognitive in nature, whereas the rest are cognitive and would not be assessed for, or considered relevant in MCT. However, in the metacognitive model the metacognitive beliefs concern specific "fusion-related" themes (Wells, 1997) that are not identified by the OCCWG. Moreover, the metacognitive approach gives importance to beliefs about rituals that are not a feature of any other approach.

Wilhelm and Steketee (2006) developed a cognitive therapy (CT) treatment manual based on the six belief groupings identified by the OCCWG and suggest that therapy should proceed by identifying which belief domain or domains are most important for each patient and modifying each one in turn in a modular approach. To illustrate how CT might proceed in modifying overestimation of danger, consider the patient who experienced an intrusion in the form of an image of her son choking on a shard of glass. A cognitive approach would advocate using the downward arrow technique to uncover fears/beliefs underpinning the patient's overestimation of the consequences of danger. In CT, the beliefs would be "I will bring glass into my house and my son will choke to death on the shard that falls from my shoe" and if that happened it would mean, "I'm a bad mother". To challenge this belief, the calculation of the probability of a dangerous outcome (van Oppen & Arntz, 1994) is undertaken, where the chance versus cumulative chance of the event is plotted. An alternative method is simply to generate a discrepancy between the patient's subjective estimate of probability and the logical probability. More simplistically, the therapist could label the thinking errors, e.g. fortune telling and catastrophizing, to reality-test the beliefs. CT might also include work on the core belief "I'm a bad mother" using continua techniques.

In MCT, none of the above beliefs are considered central to the maintenance of OCD and the use of the reattribution strategies would be contra-indicated. Clinical experience indicates that many patients conduct similar probability estimates and know that the probability of harm is infinitesimal – so why does the problem persist? The answer is that probabilistic reasoning is a form of ruminative response and/or a ritual that continues to give the intrusive thought meaning and significance. Furthermore, work on the core belief "I'm a bad mother" is unnecessary in MCT, as this thought is produced by rumination in response to the obsession. Successfully enabling the patient to suspend obsessional rumination makes it unlikely that the thought "I'm a bad mother" would occur. MCT focuses on modifying the metacognitive beliefs about the intrusion only. In this example, the metacognitive appraisal might be, "thinking that my son will choke to death means it's the case". Regardless of the nature of the obsessional thought, if the person can acquire a metacognitive mode of processing, then the thoughts no longer carry any threat. Data from several studies show that metacognitive beliefs are better predictors of obsessional symptoms than the non-metacognitive belief domains, at least in non-clinical samples (e.g. Gwilliam et al., 2004; Myers & Wells, 2005; Myers et al., 2008). A recent case series examining the efficacy of MCT for OCD supports the approach of specifically targeting metacognitive beliefs (Fisher & Wells, 2008).

Working at the metacognitive level also requires the therapist to identify and link maladaptive attentional strategies to metacognitive beliefs. A common counterproductive attentional strategy is for patients to monitor their mind and body for signs of threat. For example, an OCD patient with intrusive thoughts about harming her children described waking up each morning and scanning her mind for intrusive thoughts. This strategy was driven by the metacognitive beliefs, "I need to monitor my mind to assess my progress in therapy" and "If I don't find the thought then I know my children are safe." In this situation, the MCT therapist modifies the belief by highlighting the counterproductive nature of the strategy, i.e. that it increases the frequency and saliency of intrusive thoughts. In addition, the MCT therapist demonstrates that this attentional strategy is a manifestation of metacognitive beliefs about the importance and significance of intrusive thoughts. In this case, the patient is helped to shift to a metacognitive mode of processing and to be able to evaluate the thought objectively. This allows the patient to view the intrusive thought about hurting her children as simply a mental event that is not significant and requires no further conceptual processing. The patient was then instructed to ban these maladaptive threat monitoring strategies.

Unhelpful overt and covert coping behaviours are also components of the CAS and are driven by metacognitive beliefs about the utility of such behaviours. Typical behaviours include thought control strategies, and the way the MCT therapist works with them can be readily illustrated with reference to generalized anxiety disorder (GAD). The GAD patient often attempts to suppress thoughts that typically trigger episodes of worry. These control attempts are mostly unsuccessful and therefore contribute to the negative metacognitive belief that worrying is uncontrollable. Similarly, GAD patients often engage in avoidance behaviours that deprive them of opportunities to discover that worrying is under their control. The task of the MCT therapist is to increase the patient's awareness of the role that these coping behaviours play in fuelling negative metacognitive beliefs about uncontrollability. Subsequently, the MCT therapist assists the patient in giving up dysfunctional coping behaviours, with the goal of modifying negative metacognitive beliefs about the uncontrollable nature of worry.

Although treatment techniques within the range of CBT approaches are likely to achieve changes in metacognition, this is not the explicit goal and therapy is not conducted at the metacognitive level. For example, the logical disputation of NATs will probably increase metacognitive awareness in terms of how the person responds to her thoughts, i.e. the person begins to be aware of thoughts as mental events and not as "readouts" of reality. Indeed, Ingram and Hollon (1986) highlighted the importance of developing metacognitive awareness during cognitive therapy to enable the person to interact with their thoughts in a "decentred" manner. Although the potential importance of metacognitive change was acknowledged theoretically, treatment techniques were not explicitly developed to modify metacognitive beliefs or processes. Furthermore, metacognition was conceptualized in terms of awareness rather than as a multi-component factor in which beliefs, strategies and thinking style are important.

17

# Assessment of metacognition

A primary purpose of the assessment process is to gather information that enables the clinician to develop an idiosyncratic case formulation based on a theory or model of the particular disorder. As such, assessment is theoretically driven and the CBT therapist is interested in ascertaining the content of thinking, cognitive distortions, core beliefs and behaviours that contribute to the maintenance and exacerbation of the disorder. For example, in depressive disorders, the goal is to identify core beliefs and negative automatic thoughts that fall within the negative cognitive triad, such as "I'm a failure", "everything always goes badly" and "nothing will ever change". In relation to these cognitions, the CBT therapist looks for behaviours that prevent the individual from modifying the content of these cognitions, e.g. the belief "I'm a failure" might be maintained by avoidance and other forms of safety behaviour.

Assessment based on the metacognitive theory of psychopathology is distinctive in both its focus and methods. MCT does not ignore the behaviours and cognitions described above, but instead seeks to elicit and understand the mechanisms that generate and extend these types of thoughts and behaviours. Specifically, the MCT therapist focuses on metacognitive beliefs and processes that maintain the cognitive attentional syndrome (CAS).

Assessment in MCT will proceed in a similar fashion to other forms of therapy and typically begins from a diagnostic perspective. Once the clinician has identified the specific disorder, assessment focuses on quantifying metacognitive beliefs and processes responsible for the maintenance of the disorder.

There are three forms of assessment that are specific to MCT and each of these will now be described.

## The AMC analysis

As discussed in Point 6, the ABC analysis, common to all forms of CBT, can be reconceptualized in metacognitive terms and provides a useful starting point in the assessment process. In MCT, the "A" is normally a thought or belief, but can be an emotion. This is followed by "M", activation of a metacognitive plan, which consists of explicit metacognitive beliefs and proceduralized plans and is manifest as the CAS. In turn this leads to "C", the emotional consequences. An example of the therapist–patient dialogue in the assessment of OCD using the AMC analysis is presented below:

*Therapist*: When was the last time you had a doubt about leaving the door unlocked?

*Patient*: When I left my house this morning and was getting into my car.

*Therapist*: What exactly was the thought?

*Patient*: Did the lock click?

*Therapist*: How did you feel?

*Patient*: A little anxious and angry that the thought had happened again.

*Therapist*: What did you do in response to the thought?

*Patient*: I tried to remember the sound of the lock clicking and went through all the steps I take when locking my door.

*Therapist*: When you had the doubt about leaving the door unlocked, did that mean anything to you?

*Patient*: Well, if I've had the doubt, there must be a reason for it; these thoughts can't just come into your head for no reason.

*Therapist*: Other than going over your memory, did you do anything else?

| *Patient*: | I eventually went back and checked, as I couldn't be sure it was locked. |
| *Therapist*: | What would have happened if you'd decided not to do anything and just driven off without going back to check? |
| *Patient*: | The doubt would have stayed with me for a long time and when that happens, I can't concentrate and I get more wound up. |

In this brief example, the antecedent is the intrusive thought about leaving the door unlocked, in the form "Did the lock click?" The metacognitive plan consists of: (1) evaluating the doubt as significant and meaningful, (2) making a metacognitive judgement about the importance of thoughts intruding into consciousness, and (3) searching one's memory. The consequences included feeling anxious, angry, and ultimately checking that the door was locked.

This AMC analysis contrasts dramatically with a typical ABC analysis. In the above example, an ABC analysis would take the following form if the inflated responsibility model of OCD had been used. The antecedent or the trigger would be similar: "Have I left the door unlocked?" However, the "B", or the thought, might be: "I must check as it is my responsibility to ensure nothing bad happens." Therefore the consequences are similar in that the person goes back to check and feels anxious. However, note that the treatment target would be radically different. In the AMC analysis, we need to modify the metacognitive plan and beliefs but, in the ABC analysis, therapy would focus on modifying responsibility-related beliefs in the context of a schema model of psychopathology.

## Metacognitive profiling

Another assessment method that dovetails neatly with the AMC analysis is metacognitive profiling (Wells, 2000; Wells & Matthews, 1994). The main goal of metacognitive profiling is to elicit the nature of the processing routines and metacognitive beliefs that are activated when an individual has to deal with a stressful situation, e.g. entering a social situation for the patient with social phobia or experiencing an intrusive memory in PTSD.

Metacognitive profiling might start by asking the patient to describe a recent episode in detail and conducting the profiling as described below. Often, a more clinically useful approach is to expose the person to their feared stimulus, as is done in a Behavioural Avoidance Test (BAT), and assess for the meta-cognitive processes that are activated under such conditions.

From this point on, the assessment questions differ consider-ably from those of CBT and focus on: (1) metacognitive beliefs about thoughts, (2) metacognitive beliefs about thought control processes, and (3) the nature of the person's goals and cognitive processes in response to a stressor. These three domains are usefully subdivided into six different, but overlapping, categ-ories, which are outlined below. Example questions are included but the interested reader should refer to Wells (2000) for a detailed discussion of metacognitive profiling.

### Metacognitive beliefs and appraisals

When you felt [e.g. anxious, scared, low, angry], did you have any thoughts about your mental state? What were they?
Do you think worry/rumination can be dangerous or harmful in any way?

### Coping strategies and goals

When you felt [insert emotion], what did you do to cope with the situation/emotion?
Did you do anything to control your thoughts/emotions?
What was your goal is using these coping strategies?
What told you that your coping strategies were successful?

## Attentional processes

What were you paying most attention to in the situation?
Were you focusing on feelings/thoughts/the situation?
Were you self-conscious? What were you most conscious of?

## Memory

Did you notice any memories when in that situation?
Did you use your memory to work out what was happening or to deal with the situation?

## Judgements

How did you form your judgements in the situation?
How confident were you about your thoughts, feelings, judgements and memories?

## Mode of processing

Did you accept your thoughts/judgements as facts, based in reality?
Could you see your thoughts as unrepresentative of what was happening in the situation?
Were you able to keep your distance from the negative thoughts and feelings when they occurred?

### Metacognitive questionnaire assessment

Self-report questionnaires are used across all forms of cognitive and behavioural therapies and are important in assessing the severity of symptoms and monitoring change during and following therapy. Questionnaires are also designed to assess the putative psychological mechanisms responsible for problem maintenance. In MCT, self-report questionnaires help to determine the components of the cognitive attentional syndrome.

Administration of selected questionnaires on a session-by-session basis guides the clinician as to which metacognitive beliefs and processes should be targeted in treatment. A range of measures have been developed and used that are specific to MCT.

One of the most useful generic metacognitive questionnaires is the Metacognitions Questionnaire-30 (MCQ-30; Wells & Cartwright-Hatton, 2004), which assesses positive beliefs about worry, negative metacognitive beliefs about uncontrollability and danger of thoughts, beliefs about cognitive confidence, and cognitive self-consciousness (the tendency to monitor one's mind). There are a large number of disorder-specific questionnaires. For example, in depression, questionnaires have been designed to measure positive and negative metacognitive beliefs about rumination, as these categories of belief are pivotal in maintaining rumination and consequently depression. The specific measures are the Positive Beliefs about Rumination Scale (PBRS; Papageorgiou & Wells, 2001), which taps beliefs such as "ruminating will help me find answers to my depression". The flip-side of the coin is that negative beliefs about rumination need to be assessed with the Negative Beliefs about Rumination Scale (NBRS; Papageorgiou et al., in preparation), which measures beliefs about the uncontrollability and harmful nature of rumination, as well as beliefs about the social and interpersonal consequences of ruminating.

The use of metacognitively focused questionnaires, reformulated ABC analysis and metacognitive profiling provides the MCT therapist with a solid platform on which to build an idiosyncratic formulation based on disorder-specific metacognitive models. The focus of assessment and the resultant formulation is very different from that seen in CBT and in the "new-wave" cognitive-behavioural therapies.

# 18

# Case formulation in MCT

Case formulation plays an integral role in the delivery of empirically supported cognitive-behavioural approaches to common mental health problems. There are strong theoretical and clinical reasons for employing a case formulation approach, and MCT is no different from CBT in this regard. Case formulation provides the link between assessment and treatment and specifies the psychological constructs that need to be identified and modified over the course of therapy. The nature and construction of the case formulation is distinct in MCT, which will be illustrated here with reference to depression. The case formulation is based on the metacognitive model of depression described in Point 14. There are five main components that need to be derived for the case formulation: the trigger, the nature of rumination, positive beliefs which determine whether rumination is sustained as a response to the trigger, negative metacognitive beliefs and unhelpful coping responses. A brief example of the therapeutic dialogue is illustrated below.

## Step 1. Identifying the trigger

*Therapist*: Can you think of a recent time when you became more aware of feeling low? What was the first thing you noticed: a thought, a feeling or a particular situation?

*Patient*: It was when I was watching TV and there was a film in which the man was lonely, and I thought, he's just like me, all alone.

## Step 2. Determining the nature of rumination

*Therapist*: When you had the thought, "I'm all alone", what did you then go on to think about? [The therapist is exploring the nature of rumination.]

*Patient*: Well, I started to think that it's the same old situation. I'm sitting in here on my own watching TV, and I started to think about why I was in this situation. I ended up thinking that my life is always going to be dreadful.

*Therapist*: How long did you spend thinking about being alone and that nothing was going to change?

*Patient*: I'm not sure; quite a while. I couldn't concentrate on the rest of the programme; it could have been half an hour or maybe more.

## Step 3. Linking rumination to depression

*Therapist*: It might sound like a silly question, but when you were thinking like that, what happened to your mood?

*Patient*: Obviously it got worse. I started to feel frustrated with myself as well as feeling down.

## Step 4. Eliciting the negative metacognitive beliefs

*Therapist*: When you were feeling low and frustrated, did you have any thoughts about the way you were feeling?

*Patient*: That it was inescapable and I should be able to pull myself together.

*Therapist*: It sounds as if you spent quite a long period of time dwelling on your situation and how you were feeling. What would have happened if you hadn't spent so long thinking about your situation?

*Patient*:       I don't really know.

*Therapist*:   Well, it sounds as if your mood became worse the more you thought about yourself and your situation. It seems that as you think about your life not changing, everything seems worse. Do you think it would be helpful to stop ruminating?

*Patient*:       I really wish I could. When I start thinking about my life, I can't stop thinking about how dreadful everything is.

*Therapist*:   It sounds as if you know that ruminating about these issues is unhelpful, but that it's impossible to stop thinking about it so much.

*Patient*:       But my life is bad.

## Step 5. Discovering the positive metacognitive beliefs

*Therapist*:   Do you think ruminating in the way we just talked about will help you in any way?

*Patient*:       Not really, but sometimes I think that a way out will pop into my head if I keep thinking about it and I can work out why I'm like this.

*Therapist*:   Would there be any disadvantages or problems if you stopped dwelling on your situation?

*Patient*:       I'd probably feel better, but if I didn't think about these things I wouldn't be able to work out ways of preventing becoming depressed again.

The above information would be used to create an idiosyncratic case formulation, as shown in Figure 4. The metacognitive model of depression (Wells, 2009) has very little overlap with the cognitive theory of depression (Beck et al., 1979). In developing an MCT case formulation and in the process of MCT, minimal attention is paid to the three fundamental components

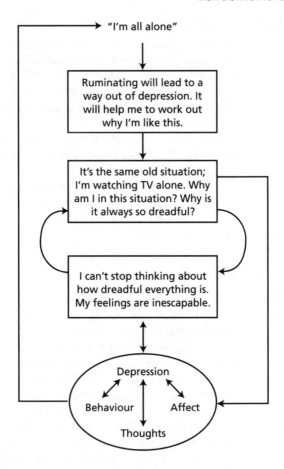

**Figure 4** Metacognitive case formulation of depression

of Beck's cognitive model. There is no detailed assessment of core beliefs (schemas), negative automatic thoughts or cognitive distortions. The MCT therapist does not completely ignore these factors, but views them as markers for the metacognitive beliefs and processes that maintain the cognitive attentional syndrome. For example, the occurrence of an NAT represents a trigger for a metacognitive plan containing positive and negative metacognitive beliefs about rumination. It is these beliefs and the ruminative process that would be addressed in MCT, not reality-testing of the NAT.

We have chosen to highlight the distinctive nature of the metacognitive case formulation for depression, but it should be noted that the case formulation for all disorders is based on the S-REF model of psychopathology and is therefore distinct from behavioural or other cognitive models of emotional disorders. Further illustrations of this can be seen in the brief overviews of the case formulation approaches for OCD and PTSD below.

In OCD, the case formulation is concerned with eliciting metacognitive beliefs about obsessions, e.g. "thinking that the house will burn down means it is the case" or "thinking I could be a paedophile makes it so". A central focus on metacognitive beliefs without drifting into cognitive appraisals is unique to MCT. In addition to these beliefs, the MCT therapist must include beliefs about rituals in the formulation. These can be either positive, "rituals give me peace of mind", or negative, "my rituals are out of control". No other approach explicitly formulates positive and negative beliefs about rituals, although such beliefs may be modified fortuitously during cognitive and behavioural interventions.

As is the case with the other disorders, the case formulation in PTSD is concerned with conveying how the cognitive attentional syndrome maintains PTSD symptoms, described in detail in Points 14 and 30. In summary, the MCT therapist highlights the fact that metacognitive beliefs about worry, rumination, threat monitoring and other coping strategies keep these processes in place, e.g. "the belief that worry keeps me safe will drive me to continue to use worry". Negative metacognitive beliefs focus on the significance of symptoms such as the belief that they are themselves a source of danger (e.g. "If I continue to think about the event I will lose my mind"). Other cognitive approaches do not emphasize the role of metacognitive beliefs in maintaining counterproductive behaviours and thinking styles and are more concerned with problems in autobiographical memory processes.

# 19

## Meta-level socialization procedures

Successfully socializing patients to the nature of therapy and the theoretical model used is crucial for effective and efficient treatment. Whatever the treatment approach, poor socialization often leads to problems in therapy because the patient is unaware of the aims of therapy and does not have a shared understanding with the therapist. MCT differs from other CBT approaches in that, regardless of the disorder being treated, the patient is socialized to the role that the cognitive attentional syndrome (see Point 3) and metacognitive beliefs play in problem maintenance.

A number of explicit socialization methods are available to the MCT therapist, but before these are described, it is important to realize that implicit socialization to the meta-cognitive model begins during the assessment phase. Self-report questionnaires, as described in Point 17, that assess metacognitive beliefs and processes are routinely administered to patients.

In addition to the useful clinical information derived from the questionnaires, it is also likely that completion of questionnaires helps to increase metacognitive awareness and attunes the patient to the goals of therapy. For example, patients often report that they hadn't thought about how much time they spent worrying or that they hadn't given consideration to the number of times they try to control thinking. The completion of specific metacognitive questionnaires helps the patient acquire an appropriate mental framework and begins the process of switching from object to metacognitive mode.

The keystone of the socialization process is the case formulation, which is the mechanism through which patients are provided with a coherent and theoretically valid framework for understanding the metacognitive processes that underpin the emotional disorder. Once the case formulation has been constructed (see Point 18 for a metacognitive formulation of depression), the task of the therapist is to illustrate carefully how each component of the formulation contributes to the maintenance of the disorder. Examples of questions the therapist should use to illustrate the effects of rumination are:

- When you ruminate, does it lead you to feeling better?
- If you described the content of your rumination, would it be positive or negative?
- Has your rumination led to a way of resolving your difficult situation?
- Does rumination ever result in action or does it lead to inaction?
- Does rumination help you to overcome and cope with your low mood?

The overarching goal in MCT is to socialize the patient to the role that the CAS plays in maintaining their current difficulties; specifically, that perseveration in the form of worry or rumination exacerbates and deepens the distress as well as prevents self-knowledge from being updated. Socialization also stresses that attentional strategies and particular coping responses prevent modification of metacognitive beliefs and contribute to a perception of threat that maintains disorder.

In relation to GAD, socialization in MCT focuses on conveying the fact that worrying is a ubiquitous phenomenon, but has become a problem for the individual because of specific positive and negative beliefs about worry and because of particular coping attempts that are counterproductive. The person is helped to see that the strategies used to try and cope with worry are unsuccessful and fuel uncontrollability beliefs. The MCT therapist highlights the conflicting nature of positive and negative beliefs about worry and enables the person to recognize that holding both types of belief leads to the maintenance of worry. To illustrate that uncontrollability and danger-related metacognitions are the central problem, a useful socialization question is: "How much of a problem would you have if you no longer believed worry was uncontrollable and dangerous?" Patients readily acknowledge that there would no longer be a problem.

In MCT for GAD (Wells, 1995, 1997), negative metacognitive beliefs about uncontrollability are the most important; these do not feature in other generic or specific models of GAD. For example, in Beck's model (Beck et al., 1985), patients are socialized to a schema model of GAD in which core beliefs about the world being a dangerous place and the self as being unable to cope are pivotal. Such beliefs drive behaviours which prevent discovery of alternative or more realistic beliefs, e.g. "I am able to cope effectively most of the time". A more specific schema theory is the intolerance of uncertainty (IOU) model (Dugas et al., 1998). In this model, patients are socialized to the idea that their perception and beliefs about the need for certainty play a fundamental role in worry and anxiety. The goal of treatment is not to eliminate uncertainty from everyday life, as this would be impossible, but to ameliorate anxiety and worry by helping the patient become more able to deal with and accept uncertain situations. The IOU model also socializes patients to the maintaining role of positive beliefs about worry but does not focus on negative beliefs about worry; instead, it focuses on problem solving and cognitive exposure.

In Point 18 on case formulation, we emphasized that MCT for OCD explicitly focuses on metacognitive beliefs about intrusions and rituals and therefore patients are socialized to the maintaining role of these beliefs. A number of cognitive models of OCD have been developed and there are some shared features. Clark (2004) argues that the similarities between cognitive approaches outweigh the differences and that all can be classified as appraisal models. It is also true that the meta-cognitive model is an appraisal theory in that interpretations of intrusions are important. However, the distinctive feature is that MCT remains focused on and socializes patients only to metacognitive processes, whereas other approaches focus on several cognitive domains, e.g. inflated responsibility, overestimation of danger and the need for certainty.

Behavioural experiments are typically used to socialize the patient to the metacognitive model. In traditional CBT approaches, thought suppression experiments are used to illustrate that this particular strategy tends to backfire and increase the frequency of unwanted thoughts. In MCT, thought suppression experiments are also used to demonstrate the counterproductive nature of thought suppression, but are also used in line with the metacognitive approach. For example, in GAD thought suppression experiments can serve multiple functions. First, they illustrate that the individual's attempt to control thoughts has fuelled the uncontrollability belief. Modifications of the thought suppression experiment are used to facilitate detached mindfulness (see Point 25). They can also be used to demonstrate that the person is consciously selecting a particular strategy in response to intrusive thoughts and therefore is able to make a different decision and choice when an intrusive thought is detected.

# 20

# Shifting to a metacognitive mode of processing

In MCT, an essential treatment goal is to help the patient change modes of processing. A fundamental feature is that the therapist needs to work at the metacognitive level explicitly and not as a byproduct as in CT. Working at the metacognitive level (see Point 16) should enable the patient to increase awareness of dysfunctional thinking styles and processes and to change their mental model of cognition and ways of experiencing thoughts.

Developing the metacognitive mode of processing consists of developing new types of awareness about mental events and processes. Patients are helped to see that the problem is not the occurrence of worrying thoughts, but that the difficulty lies in the way in which the individual relates to her internal experiences. This process begins with socialization (see Point 19) and continues with specific strategies such as detached mindfulness and modification of metacognitive beliefs.

For example, the OCD patient is in object mode and apparently has a fear of contamination by germs and dirt. However, the goal of treatment is to help the patient shift to a metacognitive mode of processing in which they see the problem as placing too much importance on their thoughts about dirt and germs. On one level, the entirety of MCT can be seen as helping the patient to acquire and shift to a metacognitive mode of experiencing.

# 21

# Modifying negative metacognitive beliefs

MCT is the only approach that explicitly focuses on modifying negative metacognitive beliefs. Negative metacognitive beliefs about thoughts or perseverative thinking can be subdivided into beliefs about worry/rumination being uncontrollable and beliefs about the danger of this thinking style. Typical uncontrollability beliefs are that worrying/ruminating is beyond control, whereas examples of danger-related beliefs include, "worrying could make me go crazy" and "people will reject me if they knew how much time I spent dwelling on my situation". During episodes of perseverative thinking, these negative beliefs are activated, leading to extended thinking and negative appraisals of worrying or ruminating, which exacerbate anxiety, depressive affect and other distressing emotions.

## *Modifying uncontrollability beliefs*

In MCT for depression and GAD, the first treatment target is the modification of beliefs concerning the uncontrollability of worry or rumination. Following the case formulation, this is accomplished by discussing the evidence for and against uncontrollability. The conundrum is put to patients that: "If worry is completely uncontrollable, how does it ever stop?" Some patients report that the worrying is never-ending, but careful questioning elicits the fact that there are significant periods when the person is not engaged in worrying or ruminating, for example when fully engaged in an absorbing task or when they are distracted from their worry. At this point, the worry/rumination postponement experiment is introduced. Patients are asked to notice a trigger for the worry/rumination such as an intrusive thought and then to simply postpone the worry/rumination until later that day. The patient is instructed that 15 minutes can be devoted to ruminating/worrying, but that this is not compulsory. This is one of the most effective strategies for challenging uncontrollability beliefs and is described in detail in Point 23. It quickly demonstrates that worry can readily and easily be brought under the individual's control.

However, worry/rumination postponement is only one way of modifying uncontrollability beliefs. The MCT therapist could utilize loss of control experiments, in which the patient is specifically requested to try and lose control of their worrying. This can be done in session or as a homework task. There is a paradoxical effect when patients conduct this experiment, as patients view their worrying as more controllable, thus demonstrating that loss of control is not possible.

In OCD, patients believe they will lose control of their thoughts or will not have peace of mind if they do not remove an obsessional doubt. In this case, the individual is asked to postpone their usual ritual (e.g. checking) to see if they lose control. This is followed by experiments such as "doubting more", to see if it is possible to lose control and in order to begin to establish an alternative relationship with intrusions.

### Modifying danger metacognitions

In MCT for GAD, individuals hold negative metacognitive beliefs about the dangers of worrying that fall into three domains: physical, social and psychological. Typical beliefs include: "worrying is harmful for my body and could lead to a heart attack", "my partner would leave me if I told her all my worries" and "worrying could make me lose my mind". Each type of belief is modified through verbal and behavioural reattribution methods. A number of verbal reattribution methods are at the MCT therapist's disposal, including:

1 Questioning the mechanism.
2 Examining the evidence that worry is harmful.
3 Reviewing counter-evidence.
4 Education and normalizing the occurrence of worry.

These verbal reattribution methods are followed up with behavioural experiments to consolidate changes in metacognitive beliefs. Specific experiments have been developed as part of MCT for GAD and include the "loss of control" experiment (Wells, 1997). For example, patients might be concerned about loss of control of their mind or behaviour. The patient is asked to try and make the feared event come true by worrying as much as possible during the allotted worry period and/or during the treatment session. This is reinforced by asking the patient to push their worries in the same way when they next notice a worry trigger in a real-life context. These experiments often serve the dual purpose of modifying both danger and uncontrollability beliefs. Similar strategies can be used across the emotional disorders, albeit with minor alterations. For example, the OCD patient might believe that obsessional rumination is uncontrollable; the worry postponement experiment can be applied in this case and can also be extended to uncontrollability beliefs about rituals.

Explicitly targeting negative metacognitive beliefs about the uncontrollability and danger of perseverative thinking is a feature unique to MCT. In GAD, no other form of cognitive or behaviour therapy directly attempts to modify negative metacognitive beliefs about the uncontrollability of worrying or danger-related metacognitions. The same is true for other disorders: in depression, CBT does not focus on negative metacognitive beliefs about the uncontrollability of rumination or the social and interpersonal consequences of engaging in rumination. Recent therapeutic developments such as behavioural activation incorporate sessions on reducing levels of rumination, but do not view the modification of negative metacognitions as the vehicle to achieve that change.

# 22

## Modifying positive metacognitive beliefs

The modification of positive metacognitive beliefs plays an integral role in MCT for all emotional disorders, as these beliefs lead the person to maintain an unhelpful coping strategy in response to unwanted thoughts and/or feelings. This can be exemplified in the case of GAD. An intrusive thought occurs, often in the form of a "what if" question (such as, "What if I fail my test?"). At this point, a person usually has a wide array of responses that can be implemented in response to this intrusion, including: (1) worrying about failing the test and the implications of failure, (2) trying to suppress the intrusive thought, (3) mental distraction, e.g. thinking about something else instead or counting backwards, (4) physical distraction, or (5) detached mindfulness, as will be seen in Point 25. However, in GAD worry is most commonly sustained as a strategy because positive metacognitive beliefs are activated about the need to worry in order to cope effectively.

Positive metacognitive beliefs are not limited to the perseverative thinking component of the CAS, as patients hold positive beliefs about attentional strategies and particular coping behaviours. For example, in PTSD and OCD, patients often hold positive beliefs about threat monitoring, e.g. "scanning the environment for signs of danger keeps me safe". Threat monitoring is not limited to external stimuli and patients often monitor for signs of anxiety, because emotion itself is often appraised as dangerous.

Modifying positive metacognitive beliefs begins with verbal reattribution. Depressed patients typically generate a broad range of positive beliefs about the function of rumination, but they typically fall into two broad domains: (1) rumination will help uncover the cause of the depression, and (2) rumination will produce an answer to how to overcome depression. Unfortunately, these erroneous positive beliefs lead the person into increasing bouts of rumination that maintain depression and solutions do not miraculously appear.

The MCT therapist conducts an advantages–disadvantages analysis and points out that there are more disadvantages than advantages to worry and rumination. The next step is to critically evaluate and challenge the advantages generated by patients, followed by exploration of whether there are better methods of achieving the advantages than via rumination. In CBT, the therapist also uses the technique of the advantages–disadvantages analysis, but this is not directed at modifying metacognitive beliefs but ordinary beliefs (e.g. "What are the disadvantages in believing you must do a perfect job?").

At times, the MCT therapist needs to ask very direct questions in order to challenge positive beliefs, e.g. "If rumination is helpful, why do you continue to have difficulties with low mood? What does this tell you about the usefulness of rumination?" This type of question can be followed up by paradoxical suggestions. For instance, the MCT therapist could state: "You might be right that rumination is helpful; maybe the problem is that you haven't spent enough time ruminating about your problems." Patients readily acknowledge that this would not be a helpful way forward. In this way, patients come to understand that rumination is not beneficial.

Other verbal reattribution strategies to modify rumination include questioning the mechanism through which rumination works and emphasizing that it generates more problems and negative mood states and rarely if ever presents solutions. Continuing on a similar theme, the MCT therapist explores the patient's goals of rumination and questions its effectiveness in achieving these goals. The task in this instance is to generate more effective alternatives for achieving goals. Another method involves the therapist exploring whether patients are employing inappropriate criteria to signal when to cease rumination, e.g.

being emotionally stable. An alternative can then be reinforced, such as the idea that an absence of rumination would more effectively achieve this goal.

Often verbal reattribution strategies go a long way to modifying positive beliefs about rumination, but it is sometimes necessary to conduct behavioural experiments to modify these beliefs. A common belief is that rumination helps to solve problems, and in order to test this belief, the patient is asked to ruminate one day, followed by minimal or no rumination the next day, and to note whether more problems were solved on the rumination day. These types of experiment are called worry/rumination modulation experiments (Wells, 2000).

Positive metacognitive beliefs about the function of worry can be modified through "mismatch strategies" (Wells, 1997). This strategy requires the patient to write down all the worries encapsulated in a specific worry episode and to compare these worries with an actual event. This can be done retrospectively as a verbal reattribution strategy or done prospectively as a behavioural experiment. In the latter case, the patient is asked to worry about a forthcoming event and a note is made of all the worries. The patient is then exposed to the feared situation and a comparison is made between the actual events and the negative predictions.

# 23

## Worry/rumination postponement

Worry and rumination occur in all emotional disorders and therefore a main therapeutic goal should be to eliminate or, at the very least, substantially reduce the amount of time an individual spends in these maladaptive thinking styles.

The worry/rumination postponement experiment is a strategy used in MCT that helps strengthen metacognitive control but principally is used to challenge metacognitive beliefs about the uncontrollability of these mental processes. It can also reduce danger-related negative metacognitive beliefs, although beliefs in this domain must also be addressed explicitly over the course of therapy.

Worry/rumination postponement begins with verbal reattribution strategies instantly recognizable to the CBT therapist. However, the target beliefs are metacognitive beliefs concerning uncontrollability, e.g. "I can't control my worrying thoughts", and not beliefs at the cognitive level, e.g. "What if I lose my job?" The MCT therapist reviews with the patient the evidence for and against the uncontrollable nature of worry and rumination to demonstrate that perseverative thinking can be controlled (see Point 21 for more details on verbal reattribution of negative metacognitive beliefs). Following verbal reattribution, the worry/rumination postponement is introduced with an appropriate rationale, as illustrated below:

We have discussed the important role that your belief that worry is uncontrollable plays in keeping your worry and anxiety in place. One of the reasons you believe worry is uncontrollable is because you have had so few experiences of successfully interrupting your worrying. Unfortunately, when you have tried to stop worrying, the strategies you've used, such as attempting not to think about a specific topic, have not worked very well. Using this type of strategy has actually fuelled your belief that worrying is uncontrollable. So I would like you to try a different way of responding to your worries when they occur.

Patients are then given the following explicit instructions:

When you notice a worry pop into your mind, I'd like you to say to yourself, "Stop; this is only a thought, I'm not going to engage with it now, I'll leave it alone and worry about it later." Allocate a time later in the day, when you will allow yourself 15 minutes to worry. When that time arrives, you can engage in your postponed worry, and worry as much as you want to. However, you don't have to use this worry period and most people choose not to use it as they have either forgotten about the worry or prefer not to do it. However, if you do decide to use the worry period, please make a note of why you decided to use it. This is an experiment to find out how much control you really have over your worry.

One very important feature of this experiment is that the therapist must make a clear distinction between worry postponement and thought suppression. Patients are not being asked to rid themselves of the content of unwanted thoughts; instead, they are being asked to suspend any further processing of the initial thought. The therapist should monitor changes in degree of conviction that worry is uncontrollable.

Although the worry/rumination postponement experiment increases awareness of the pervasive nature of worry or rumination, the MCT therapist undertakes a detailed review of the breadth of application to ensure that the patient is applying the strategy to the majority of instances of perseverative thinking. At times, patients are resistant to postponing rumination or worry due to strongly held positive beliefs about the usefulness of worry/rumination. In such instances, the therapist's task is to use verbal and behavioural reattribution methods to modify such positive metacognitive beliefs (see Point 22).

In MCT, worry postponement is used to challenge uncontrollability and limit the CAS. Controlled worry periods have been used in other treatment approaches for GAD (e.g. Borkovec et al., 1983). However, the MCT approach differs from such stimulus control applications. Stimulus control is based on the assumption that patients have lost discriminative control over the worry process; postponed worry periods are designed to enable patients to regain control over worry. In MCT, it is not assumed that there is any actual loss of control; instead, beliefs about control are erroneous.

Borkovec and colleagues ask individuals to utilize postponed worry periods during which they "problem solve" their worries. This is not a feature of MCT, since problem solving of individual concerns is contra-indicated as another example of extended reasoning about thought content. As described above, in MCT the use of the postponed worry period is optional and used later in treatment. Then, the patient actually tries to lose control of their worry in order to further modify uncontrollability beliefs and beliefs about the dangerous nature of worry.

# 24

# Attention training technique

A primary goal of MCT is to reduce self-focused processing and enhance metacognitive control, which can be achieved through a specific strategy called the Attention Training Technique (ATT; Wells, 1990). ATT comprises three externally focused auditory attentional tasks: selective attention, attention switching and divided attention tasks. These are conducted sequentially during a 10–15-minute ATT session. Selective attention is practised for approximately five minutes before the next step of rapid attention switching for five minutes. The final step of ATT is a two-minute divided attention component.

The term *attention training* is often referred to in the new generation of cognitive-behavioural approaches and should not be confused with ATT. For example, Acceptance and Commitment Therapy (ACT; Hayes et al., 1999) incorporates training in self-directed attention, with the goal of sustained exposure to emotions thereby leading to desensitization of the conditioned response and the reversal of avoidance behaviour. The purpose of ATT is not to sustain exposure to unwanted emotions but to develop greater executive control. In Mindfulness Based Cognitive Therapy (MBCT; Segal et al., 2002), reference is also made to attention training. But in this instance it refers to the redeployment of attention as a component of meditation. Specifically, patients are asked, if they notice an unwanted thought during meditative practice, to reallocate their focus to their breathing. In this way, patients treated with MBCT remain self-focused, whereas ATT is designed to counteract excessive self-focus and utilizes only external focusing. ATT is not applied in response to thoughts or emotions. It is not a coping technique but a training exercise that is intended to build the necessary framework and procedures for improving metacognitive control over processing.

A summary description of ATT, as outlined by Wells (2000, 2009), is presented below.

## Step 1: Introducing ATT

ATT begins by providing the patient with a credible and understandable rationale for the treatment technique. The unifying theme across disorders is that excessive self-focus leads to an increase in the saliency and severity of symptoms, but the rationale is tailored to the specific presenting problem. Self-focus here is used as a short-hand label for the CAS. In panic disorder and health anxiety, the therapist stresses that focusing on bodily symptoms plays a crucial maintaining factor, whereas in depression, patients are helped to see that the tendency to be attentive to thoughts and feelings is associated with rumination, thereby exacerbating and maintaining low mood. Socialization experiments are used to highlight how excessive self-focus and rumination maintain and exacerbate the patient's presenting problem. The case formulation is used to highlight the association between excessive self-focused attention and the presenting problem.

Once the patient has a good understanding of the maintaining role of excessive self-focus, the therapist introduces ATT. Credibility of the technique should be assessed and, if there is low credibility, then further work is undertaken to socialize the patient to the role that maladaptive attentional strategies play in problem maintenance.

## Step 2: Self-focus ratings

Before implementing ATT, the patient's current level of self-focus versus external focus is assessed using a simple Likert scale. This rating is repeated after implementing ATT. The scale provides an index of change following the ATT procedure; a two-point change in level of self-focus is normally required and, if the change is less than this, the reasons are explored and ATT potentially re-administered.

## Step 3: Implementation of ATT

Before ATT starts, the therapist emphasizes that the task is to practise focusing attention as guided. A crucial instruction is that, should intrusive thoughts or feelings occur, the task is simply to treat these thoughts or feelings as background noise and not attempt to suppress or remove them.

ATT begins with the auditory selective task. The therapist instructs the patient throughout the procedure and guides the patient to attend to at least three sounds in the room, such as the therapist's voice, the ticking of a clock or the hum of a computer. Next, the patient is instructed to attend sequentially to three other sounds or spatial locations outside the consulting room. Once six to eight sounds have been identified and selectively attended to, the therapist instructs the patient to switch their attention rapidly between the different sounds. These stages are each conducted for five to six minutes. The final stage is to instruct the patient in a divided attention task, which requires them to attempt to listen to all the sounds simultaneously; this is practised for two to three minutes. Throughout the task, the MCT therapist ensures that the patient finds the task relatively difficult, i.e. attention demands are high.

## Step 4: Review ATT and set homework

After practising ATT the theorist reviews the procedure with the patient and plans how it will be implemented for homework. Patients are asked to complete ATT at least once per day for 15 minutes, but are reminded that it should not be used as a coping strategy, e.g. to distract themselves from unwanted thoughts and feelings.

ATT has been shown to be associated with symptom improvements and changes in worry and beliefs in a range of disorders, including panic disorder (Wells, 1990; Wells et al., 1997), major depressive disorder (Papageorgiou & Wells, 2000) and health anxiety (Cavanagh & Franklin, 2001; Papageorgiou & Wells, 1998). In addition, the first case study of ATT for auditory hallucinations was recently completed (Valmaggia et al., 2007). See Wells (2007) for a review of the effects of ATT.

# 25

# Implementing detached mindfulness

MCT aims to promote "detached mindfulness" (DM; Wells & Matthews, 1994), which counteracts the cognitive attentional syndrome. Detached mindfulness refers to how individuals respond to mental events (e.g. worries, intrusive images, negative thoughts, and memories). As described in Point 7, detached mindfulness involves discontinuation of any further cognitive or coping response to thoughts, which typically involves the suspension of perseverative thinking and specific coping strategies such as focusing, avoidance or transforming thoughts. The second feature of detachment consists of an individual directly experiencing self as an observer separate from the occurrence of the thought itself.

## Application of detached mindfulness in MCT

The overall treatment goal of MCT is to promote detached mindfulness and therefore most treatment strategies available to the MCT therapist contribute to the development of this state. However, several specific techniques have been developed that facilitate detached mindfulness (Wells, 2005). Described below are two of these techniques.

## Free association task

This task has multiple goals, including developing meta-awareness, low levels of conceptual processing and detachment. The task can be presented following a discussion of the natural flow and decay of emotionally neutral thoughts over the course of a typical day facilitated by simple questions, such as "What happens to the majority of your everyday thoughts? Where do these thoughts go?" Patients quickly come to realize that for the vast majority of their thoughts, "detached mindfulness" is the natural processing state; it is only the intrusive thoughts that are volitionally allocated attention and sustained processing that become problematic. The next step is to convey that intrusive thoughts are no different from other thoughts and therefore it is entirely possible to choose not to engage with intrusive thoughts. The task itself is then introduced as a means of developing experiential (procedural) knowledge to support the state:

> In a moment I am going to say a list of common words and I would like you to let your mind roam freely in response to the words. It's important that you do not attempt to control your mind or your response to the words; I just want you to passively notice what happens in your mind. For some people, not much happens, other people find that pictures or images come into their mind and some people also report feelings or sensations. I'm now going to say the list of common words: orange, pen, table, tiger, trees, glasses, breeze, statue. What happened when you just watched your mind?

Patients typically report that as each word is spoken, an image of that word occurs. Often these are discrete images, each replacing the previous one, but sometimes images merge together or no thought occurs. The natural ebb and flow of thoughts is pointed out by asking what happened to the first thought as the task proceeded. Patients come to see that thoughts decay without the need to attempt to remove them or process them in an extended way. Repeating the procedure and asking the patient to become aware of the self as a separate observer of the thoughts enhance detachment.

Detached mindfulness in response to intrusions and other classes of unwanted thought can be further facilitated by including emotionally salient words in this task. The central idea is that patients can simply notice thoughts and not get caught up in further processing of them. Patients are asked to apply the strategy of passively noticing their negative thoughts, worries, intrusions and feelings for homework.

## Tiger task

This task provides patients with the experience of DM, by bringing an image of a tiger to mind and simply watching the image without attempting to influence the image. The therapist assists this process with the following instructions:

> In order to get a feel for using detached mindfulness, I'd like you to begin by bringing an image of a tiger to mind. I don't want you to try and influence the image, so don't try to change the tiger's behaviour or change anything about it. The image might be in black and white or colour; it doesn't matter, just notice the tiger. The tiger might move, but don't make it move; just watch how the image develops over time, but do not try to influence it; simply watch the image of the tiger in a passive way.

These tasks are practised in session, but can also be used as homework tasks to promote detached mindfulness. The ultimate goal for patients is to "do nothing" upon noticing an intrusive thought, whether it occurs in the form of a worry, a negative automatic thought, an obsession, an aversive memory or an image. In MCT, detached mindfulness is used in conjunction with worry/rumination postponement to facilitate low levels of perseverative thinking, to modify maladaptive attentional strategies and remove dysfunctional coping behaviours. In other words, the implementation of detached mindfulness limits the cognitive attentional syndrome and reduces psychopathology.

Recent innovations in cognitive approaches to treating emotional disorders, such as Mindfulness Based Cognitive Therapy (MBCT; Segal et al., 2002) and Acceptance and Commitment Therapy (ACT; Hayes et al., 1999), use the term "mindfulness" in describing their theories and treatment strategies. However, "mindfulness" is distinct from "detached mindfulness" as specified in MCT. The use of similar terms has caused confusion in clinicians' minds, with the two constructs often viewed synonymously, but parallels should not be drawn simply on the basis of terminological similarities.

Mindfulness is defined as "paying attention in a particular way; on purpose, in the present moment and non judgmentally" (Kabat-Zinn, 1994: 4). Over the past two decades, interest in the concept of mindfulness has burgeoned and has been incorporated into a range of clinical approaches. Mindfulness was first utilized by Kabat-Zinn (1982), in his Mindfulness Based Stress Reduction (MBSR) programme, as a treatment package for patients with chronic pain, but has subsequently been used for a range of behavioural and emotional difficulties (Kabat-Zinn, 1998). In this context, the state of mindfulness is achieved through various Buddhist meditation exercises (Hanh, 1976). MBCT combines cognitive therapy with mindfulness meditation practice, whereas ACT develops mindfulness through many different treatment components, including acceptance, cognitive defusion, willingness, focusing on the present moment and attentional training (Masuda et al., 2004).

A brief foray into the application of mindfulness as used in ACT and MBCT illuminates the differences from detached mindfulness. Roemer and Orsillo (2002) suggest that the integration of mindfulness and acceptance practices would enhance the efficacy of CBT for GAD and have included elements of mindfulness in their approach (Roemer & Orsillo, 2007). Mindful practices in ACT include imagining leaves floating down a stream and attempting to place thoughts, feelings and experiences on the leaves and watch them float away. This strategy is not the same as DM because it entails further processing in the form of doing something with the thoughts. In MCT, this could be used as a metaphor to explain that thoughts are fleeting events that do not require attention, but not as a specific exercise as it is essentially a thought control strategy. Progressive muscle relaxation is conceptualized as a method of promoting mindfulness, rather than a method of controlling anxiety in Roemer and Orsillo's acceptance-based behaviour therapy for GAD. This treatment strategy is not applied in MCT.

Another treatment component of ACT designed to promote mindfulness is termed "cognitive defusion". ACT utilizes many different strategies under this umbrella term. One specific method, called deliteralization, refers to removing the literal content of the thought, thereby enabling the client to take a non-judgemental stance on their thoughts with greater willingness and acceptance. Physicalizing is an example of a deliteralization strategy, in which the patient ascribes colours or shapes to the intrusive thought. This stands in stark contrast to detached mindfulness, in which the central component is the absence of further processing in the form of transformation in response to thoughts. Also, the clinical target of the above strategy is the thought that intrudes into consciousness, not the beliefs (or plans) that drive conceptual processing, as in MCT. Furthermore, detached mindfulness in MCT is used as a component of behavioural experiments to modify uncontrollability beliefs, which is not a specific goal of other mindfulness techniques.

As previously mentioned, MBCT is an integration of cognitive therapy strategies and mindfulness meditation. A range of meditative exercises is included in each treatment session and given for homework. Exercises include mindful eating, during which the therapist and patient slowly eat raisins, focusing their attention on aspects of eating as well as on their thoughts and emotions. A body scan is introduced where the patient is instructed to focus his attention on different parts of his body and is encouraged to view any sensations in a non-judgemental manner. If unwanted thoughts occur, the patient is asked to return his attention to his body. Other forms of meditative exercises included are mindful stretching, mindful walking and sitting meditation, where awareness is focused on breathing and patients are asked to refocus their attention on their breathing should it be captured by thoughts, feelings or experiences. A generalization strategy is also included, which is the use of a brief three-minute breathing space to cultivate mindfulness during the day. This strategy can also be used in response to symptoms of anxiety or other unwanted feelings or thoughts. This requires the patient to allocate attention away from triggering stimuli and to refocus on their breath. MCT does not employ any of these strategies; indeed, responding to intrusive thoughts or feelings by redirecting attention away from the aversive experiences runs contrary to the aims of MCT, as doing so may maintain erroneous metacognitive beliefs about the need to respond to thoughts and feelings.

Clearly, mindfulness meditative practices call upon meta-cognitive processes and beliefs because they involve the allocation of attention and control of cognition. However, these procedures have not been developed in the context of a model of metacognition and psychopathology. The goals of the techniques, unlike the goal of DM, are not operationalized in metacognitive terms and they impact potentially on a wide range of factors, all of which may not be beneficial. For instance, it is noteworthy that mindfulness meditation uses strategies that increase body focus as a means of moving attention away from thoughts.

# 26

# Situational attentional refocusing

Situational attentional refocusing (SAR; Wells, 2000; Wells & Papageorgiou, 1998) is a treatment strategy designed to reverse the current maladaptive attentional strategies a person adopts in a stressful context. Although the types of attentional strategy may vary between patients and across disorders, maladaptive attentional strategies prevent the person from modifying their knowledge. Typical dysfunctional attentional strategies include both excessive self-focus seen in social phobia and inappropriate threat monitoring that so often characterizes PTSD or OCD.

In social phobia, the individual engages in self-focused processing when exposed to a feared social situation, which is guided by positive metacognitive beliefs concerning the utility of self-focus. In addition to focusing on signs and symptoms of anxiety, individuals allocate attention to a self-generated image of how they believe they appear to other people, i.e. from an observer's perspective. In this constructed image, the signs of anxiety are viewed as extremely conspicuous and exaggerated. For example, the social phobic may blush, which in reality is barely noticeable; in the image of the mind's eye, however, the person views herself as "burning up" and being the colour of beetroot. This self-focus interferes with the processing of external features of the social environment, so the person fails to learn that they are not really conspicuous and the centre of everyone's attention. Self-focus also increases awareness and severity of anxiety, and reduces performance in social situations.

SAR strategies allow the MCT therapist to reduce excessive self-focus and allow new information to be incorporated in processing routines. In the case of social phobia, this means enabling the person to shift to focusing their attention externally rather than remaining self-focused. For example, patients with social phobia often express the concern that people stare at them in social situations. A patient commented that when she entered a bar, everyone turned and looked at her. The therapist asked how she knew this to be true as she typically avoided eye contact in social situations. Instead, she would focus her attention on how she was feeling and the negative image in her mind. Behavioural experiments involving directing attention externally rather than internally allowed the person to incorporate new knowledge. Therefore, in the above example, the behavioural experiment simply consisted of focusing attention externally on other people in the environment in order to facilitate belief change.

Similar dysfunctional attentional strategies are evident in PTSD and are also guided by positive metacognitive beliefs about the helpful nature of such strategies. For example, patients are frequently hypervigilant for threat, driven by the belief that "checking for danger keeps me safe". The therapist helps reorient the person's attention on to neutral stimuli and safety signals in the environment. In this way, the "danger and threat programme" is taken off-line and cognition is allowed to tune back to a pre-trauma routine.

# 27

# Targeting meta-emotions

Meta-emotion is emotion about emotion or emotion applied to regulating emotion or used as a reference point for coping. Patients often use emotions as a source of metacognitive information that contributes to the maintenance of the psychological disorder. In the S-REF model (see Point 2), the information derived from positive and negative emotional states contributes to appraisals of thoughts and of self-knowledge and is used to indicate whether continued coping efforts are required. For example, in GAD, when an intrusive thought in the form of a "what if" question occurs, self-focused attention increases, the worry process begins and the person uses their emotional state, i.e. reduction in anxiety, as a cue to when to cease worrying.

Meta-emotions clearly overlap with the construct of emotional reasoning, in which beliefs such as "I feel worthless therefore I am worthless" or "I feel hopeless therefore the future is hopeless" operate and are addressed in cognitive therapy. A closely related construct is ex-consequentia reasoning (Arntz et al., 1995), in which emotions are perceived as indicators of threat, in the form of: "If I feel anxious, then there must be danger." However, Wells (2000) argues that the concept of meta-emotions extends beyond these forms of systematic errors or biased thinking and instead represents internal information that regulates cognition and coping strategies.

The MCT therapist pays careful attention to meta-emotional states. In depression, patients are often hypersensitive to potential signs of depression and/or recurrence of the problem and will interpret any symptoms in a negative way as indicating relapse. This style of responding can reactivate the CAS in patients, i.e. the patient will then engage in rumination, increase the level of self-monitoring and resort to avoidance. For example, a depressed patient described having a very good week, but then questioned this mood state and began to ruminate on how long "the good mood" would last, with the resultant effect of a rapid deterioration in mood. In addition, the same patient had anxiety about positive emotional states (meta-emotion), as these were regarded as transitory and meant that, when her mood dipped, the decreases would be so dramatic as to make the subsequent depressive episodes unbearable. Indeed, this patient expressed her preference for maintaining a relatively flat affect (meta-emotion), as this would avoid large fluctuations in mood. This is a metacognitive process in which the patient selected a particular emotional state volitionally. In this instance, the therapist modifies the metacognitive beliefs driving the strategy and normalizes mood fluctuations. Patients can be asked what happens to the emotions, e.g. "Do they continue for ever or do they fluctuate?" or "Have you ever experienced an emotion that has lasted for ever?" Clearly, the answer is no, and by not engaging with the emotion, the patient would learn that emotions rapidly fade and are replaced by other emotional states.

The premise that an individual is volitionally selecting a particular mood state or is fearful of emotion can be readily understood in the context of a metacognitive framework, but is not readily conceptualized in other forms of therapy. However, recent work on emotional schemas (e.g. Leahy, 2007) that has been stimulated by the S-REF model has begun to explore the idea that beliefs about emotions may be important in CBT.

# 28

# Delivering metacognitively focused exposure

Exposure is a fundamental feature of all cognitive and behavioural interventions, including MCT. However, exposure in behaviour therapy, cognitive therapy and MCT is based on distinct theoretical constructs that translate into different forms and applications of exposure in therapy. The use of exposure is important in both assessment (see Point 17) and treatment.

In MCT, exposure is used primarily in the form of a brief behavioural experiment, which is presented with a specific theoretical rationale designed to test and change metacognitive beliefs and processes. As MCT treats disorders through modification of the cognitive attentional syndrome, it is not predicated on a behavioural model of anxiety. This means that MCT does not rely on extensive exposure, as is the case in exposure and response prevention for OCD, or imaginal or in-vivo exposure to traumatic images/memories in PTSD.

Exposure is used in MCT in a number of ways, but this discussion will focus on just two: (1) the modification of metacognitive beliefs, and (2) the facilitation of adaptive processing in trauma.

Modification of metacognitive beliefs requires the therapist to identify and test positive and negative metacognitive beliefs about thinking, as illustrated by the following therapist–patient dialogue in a case of OCD:

*Therapist*:  What do you think will happen when you have thoughts about hurting your son?

*Patient*:  That I might end up acting on those thoughts and hurt my son and he'll be taken into care.

| *Therapist*: | Do you try to control these thoughts in any way? |
| *Patient*: | I try not to have them by avoiding contact with my son when my husband isn't here. When I'm alone with my son, I almost always get the thoughts. I also change the image I have of hurting my son into one where I'm playing with him. |
| *Therapist*: | What do you think would happen if you no longer avoided being alone with your son and didn't change the intrusive thought into a positive image? |
| *Patient*: | I'd hurt my son, if I didn't get rid of the thought. |
| *Therapist*: | It sounds like you believe these thoughts are really important. Do you think having thoughts about hurting your son will lead you to doing so? |
| *Patient*: | Yes, I really don't want to have them. |
| *Therapist*: | How much do you believe that having the image of hurting your son could make you do it? |
| *Patient*: | Quite a lot when I have the image and I'm alone with my son; I guess about 70 per cent. |
| *Therapist*: | So it seems that you are giving these thoughts considerable importance. What we need to do is help you recognize that these thoughts are insignificant and meaningless. |

This patient was asked to interact with her son and postpone her thought control strategies and coping behaviours to test the metacognitive belief: "Thinking that I will hurt my son will make me do it." She was asked to do this under two conditions: first, to respond when the intrusions spontaneously occurred and, second, to deliberately invoke the obsession and keep it in mind for two to three minutes whilst playing with her son, and then to continue to postpone her neutralizing strategies. This approach is different from that taken from the behavioural perspective, which focuses predominantly on enabling the person to habituate to the anxiety and would require substantially greater periods of time (several hours) than the two to three minutes used in the above metacognitively focused behavioural experiment. The behavioural approach might expose the patient to a recording of her thought. Specifically, that she repeatedly listens to the thought whilst not engaging in any neutralizing behaviours. Prolonged and repeated exposure of this kind would not be a feature of MCT. The aim of CBT is to promote habituation to the intrusion, but the aim in MCT is to challenge the metacognitive belief about the intrusion and allow the patient to relate to it in new ways. Therefore, therapy should be conducted solely at the metacognitive rather than the cognitive or behavioural level. Fisher and Wells (2005) demonstrated that brief exposure and response prevention (ERP) presented with a metacognitive rationale was more effective than ERP presented with a behavioural (habituation) rationale in OCD patients.

A second use of exposure in MCT is in the treatment of PTSD, in which metacognitively delivered exposure aims to reduce and replace dysfunctional processing and coping behaviours. Instead of responding to intrusive thoughts and memories with perseverative thinking and counterproductive coping strategies, patients are instructed to respond to these cognitive events using detached mindfulness. The rationale given to patients is that unhelpful strategies such as worry, rumination, avoidance and hypervigilance are preventing normal adaptive processing of symptoms resulting from a traumatic experience. MCT for PTSD is discussed in detail in Points 14 and 30. The distinctive nature of this treatment approach is that it does not require repeated and prolonged exposure to trauma memories; therefore, patients are never asked to write or narrate detailed accounts of their traumas. Instead, patients are instructed merely to notice the intrusions and desist from further conceptual processing, i.e. abandon thought control and perseverative thinking. In-vivo exposure can be a component of treatment but only to the extent that patients are asked to return to their usual pre-trauma routine if appropriate and to abandon maladaptive strategies of threat monitoring in these situations (e.g. Wells & Sembi, 2004a).

# 29

# Developing new plans for processing

The metacognitive model proposes that the CAS is linked to the priming of dysfunctional processing plans, in response to unwanted thoughts, feelings or events. For example, in depression, the metacognitive plan and associated metacognitive beliefs might be: "I need to ruminate in order to find a way out of depression", "My sadness is uncontrollable" and "Negative thoughts are important and must be attended to". Therefore each time a negative thought or mood deviation intrudes into consciousness, the person effectively "downloads" a plan from long-term memory, resulting in prolonged and sustained rumination. A goal of the MCT therapist is to modify this plan. Each aspect of MCT is designed to enable the patient to develop and select an appropriate alternative plan that limits the CAS, thereby ameliorating psychopathology.

In general, developing a new plan for processing is an explicit focus of the latter stages of MCT. This functions as a relapse prevention strategy designed to reduce vulnerability to future episodes of prolonged emotional disturbance. Construction of the new plan begins with a detailed account of the patient's old plan. The new or replacement plan consists of selecting the opposite attentional strategies and coping behaviours and an absence of perseverative thinking. Outlined in Figure 5 is an example of an old plan and the new plan for an OCD patient with contamination fears about toxic materials.

The MCT therapist enables the patient to practise the new plan frequently in a range of situations. For the OCD patient illustrated in Figure 5, this included brief exposures (five minutes) to feared situations and implementation of the new plan. As described in Point 28, the goal is not habituation, as in

| Plan A (old plan) | Plan B (new plan) |
|---|---|
| 1 Pay attention to intrusions | 1 Apply detached mindfulness to intrusions |
| 2 Give meaning and significance to intrusions | 2 Tolerate initial anxiety/distress when intrusions occur |
| 3 Scan environment for signs of dirt and broken glass | 3 Ban scanning the environment |
| 4 Avoid the cleaning zones of supermarket | 4 Do not avoid any situations |
| 5 Tell self not to be stupid in response to doubts | 5 Don't engage in thought control strategies |
| 6 Try to mentally distract self from thoughts | 6 Desist from analytical reasoning |
| 7 Try to remove intrusions from consciousness | 7 If wash hands in response to intrusion, keep intrusion in mind rather than attempting to banish the intrusion |
| 8 Calculate probability of harm coming to children | |
| 9 Monitor mind for intrusions | |
| 10 Wash hands without having the intrusion | |

**Figure 5** Example of an old plan and new plan for an OCD patient with contamination fears

behaviour therapy, but modification of repeated dysfunctional processing guided by metacognitive beliefs. Practising the new plan is not limited to homework tasks; it should be implemented in therapy each time the therapist notices activation of the maladaptive plan, e.g. occurrences of perseverative thinking or inappropriate threat monitoring. In other words, the MCT therapist is working at the metacognitive level and not the cognitive level when developing and helping patients to implement new processing.

Development of the new plan includes a discussion of fears of recurrence and anticipated problems in the future. The fear of recurrence often involves a particular plan for processing that is problematic. A common maladaptive response strategy used by patients with OCD is to continue to monitor the stream of consciousness in order to check for an absence of negative thoughts. This constitutes a maladaptive plan, which should be highlighted and modified. In a similar fashion, discussion regarding future possible stressful situations and how the patient imagines dealing with these situations also elicits counterproductive processing plans and erroneous metacognitive beliefs. Practice and rehearsal help to reduce vulnerability by consolidating alternative plans for processing.

# 30

# Integrating MCT techniques: a case study

In this final section, a case study of MCT for PTSD is presented. This case study illustrates how MCT combines the distinctive practical and theoretical features into a coherent and novel treatment. The treatment described is based on two treatment manuals (Wells, 2009; Wells & Sembi, 2004a).

Sadie arrived home one evening and was attacked by three young men as she got out of her car. She tried to prevent the theft of her car, but as she struggled with one of her attackers, she became entangled in the seat belt and was dragged down the road as the car was driven off. Consequently, she suffered a number of leg injuries and substantial lacerations to her upper body and face. After this traumatic incident, Sadie developed PTSD and had been experiencing symptoms for approximately two years. The main PTSD symptoms were repeated intrusive memories of the incident and a strong sense of re-experiencing the event in which she would feel disconnected from reality and could hear the sound of the car's roaring engine and feel the burning pain in her legs as if the event were happening again. Up to three hours per day were spent worrying and ruminating. Worry primarily focused on the possibility of a similar event happening again in the future, whereas the rumination centred on her inability to prevent the theft. As a direct consequence of the PTSD symptoms, Sadie felt that her life had been taken away. Her once thriving small business was on the point of collapse because she often avoided leaving her home. Not surprisingly, there were marked levels of depression and anxiety.

In the first treatment session, the nature and rationale of MCT for PTSD was presented to Sadie. The therapist explained that it is "normal" to experience such symptoms in the aftermath of a traumatic event and, in fact, these symptoms are a necessary part of an adaptation process. However, trauma-related symptoms normally fade over time, but unfortunately the symptoms can inadvertently be maintained when people use particular coping strategies. Fortunately, it is relatively straightforward to identify these unhelpful coping strategies and replace them with helpful behaviours and responses to the unwanted thoughts and memories.

The therapist carefully conducted a focused assessment in order to identify the metacognitive beliefs, processes and coping strategies and construct an idiosyncratic case formulation based on the metacognitive model of PTSD (see Point 14). As previously noted, Sadie was spending a great deal of time ruminating and worrying. There had also been a substantial change in her attentional processes; she was aware of being very vigilant for signs of threat whenever she left the house and also frequently checked her body for signs of anxiety.

To uncover the metacognitive beliefs underpinning perseverative thinking, the therapist explored why Sadie believed that worrying about a similar event occurring was helping and what advantages were gained by repeatedly examining the event from many different angles. Sadie was also asked about the advantages of looking out for signs of threat in her environment and her body.

The main positive metacognitive belief elicited about worry was: "Worrying about the event happening again means I can take action to avoid it and ensure that I am safe at all times." In terms of rumination, the belief was: "Examining what happened from all angles means I can work out why it happened and then I can stop thinking about it and be happy again." Her negative metacognitive beliefs about worry and rumination were: "When I start thinking about the event, I can't stop" and "If I can't stop going over the event, I'll go mad." Her metacognitive beliefs about threat monitoring were: "If I look around me for threat then I can make sure I'll be safe" and "Noticing that I'm anxious makes me alert for danger and I won't be caught out."

The metacognitive model of PTSD also specifies a number of additional unhelpful coping strategies that prevent the person escaping from unhelpful conceptual processing. Accordingly, the therapist assessed for such strategies and found that Sadie was checking the doors and windows repeatedly in an attempt to control her anxiety. She also avoided being out of her own house after dark, and tried to control her thoughts by transforming the aversive memories. Instead of becoming injured, in her memory she tried to imagine capturing the assailants and gaining retribution. This strategy was driven by the metacognitive belief: "If I don't get rid of the images, I'll go mad." These strategies were included in the case formulation, as illustrated in Figure 6.

The case formulation was shared with Sadie as the first step in socialization (Point 19) to the metacognitive approach. Sadie was helped to understand that the strategies listed above were maintaining and exacerbating her trauma symptoms, as well as increasing her levels of anxiety and depression. In order to accomplish this goal and to give Sadie an appropriate mental framework for understanding the aims of MCT, the therapist used the "healing metaphor":

Your body has an inbuilt method of repairing itself; for example, if you cut your hand the body heals itself, you don't have to do anything to heal the cut. Your mind is no different; it too has an inbuilt mechanism for healing itself. Let's imagine you have a wound. Leaving it alone and doing nothing to it is the best thing you can do; if you keep interfering with the wound it will slow down the healing process. Your intrusive memories and other symptoms are like a wound and it's best to leave them to their own devices. Worrying or ruminating about your intrusive thoughts and memories, trying to control thoughts and control your attention is like interfering with the wound. You must allow

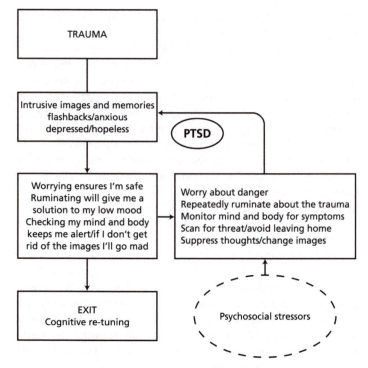

**Figure 6** Metacognitive case formulation of PTSD

the healing process to take care of itself and you'll find that the emotional wound will fade.

The socialization process was completed by asking Sadie a series of questions to help her understand the problems inherent in using worry and other unhelpful coping strategies in response to her intrusive thoughts. For example, "Does worrying lead to you feeling safe?" and "Does focusing attention on signs of danger help you to have an accurate view of how dangerous situations actually are?" The therapist then used a behavioural experiment to illustrate the rebound effect of thought suppression, followed by training in detached mindfulness using a free association task (Points 7 and 25). The detached mindfulness state was contrasted with the effects of thought control, before implementing the worry/rumination postponement exercise as homework.

Sadie reported a reasonably high degree of success in implementing detached mindfulness to the negative thoughts, intrusive memories and images. The postponed worry/rumination period was never used, as Sadie felt it unnecessary. However, she had engaged with approximately 40 per cent of her intrusive thoughts, which she labelled as the "worst images". Using metacognitive profiling (see Point 17), it was determined that her goal was to remove these thoughts from memory and she was searching for methods to achieve this. In other words, the occurrence of the most distressing thoughts activated the metacognitive belief: "I need to ruminate in order to find a way of getting rid of these images." The MCT therapist discussed this strategy in reference to the case formulation and reiterated the counterproductive nature of this strategy. Sadie was asked to bring the worst image to mind and to practise detached mindfulness. To her surprise, Sadie experienced only a brief period of anxiety in response to this exercise and found that the thought faded rapidly. She was encouraged to continue with detached mindfulness for homework and to apply the worry/rumination postponement to all forms of unwanted thought.

Therapy moved on to modifying the attentional strategies contributing to problem maintenance. Sadie was asked how she worked out what she needed to pay attention to in order to be safe. She stated that she needed to scan the environment and repeatedly ask herself "Is it safe?", followed by "What if it isn't safe?", and then generate reasons for and against. The therapist identified that this was another example of worrying and should be banned. Through further questioning, Sadie realized that she wasn't paying attention to signs of safety in the environment. This was illustrated starkly over the course of the following week, when she had been instructed to focus her attention in a balanced way. Whilst driving, she was stationary at a set of traffic lights and noticed three young men wearing similar clothing to that of her attackers. Previously, this would have acted as a trigger for worry and intrusive memories and a series of maladaptive attentional strategies. Instead, she scanned her environment more fully and noticed that there was a police car behind her. This slightly fortuitous event provided a clear illustration of how simply focusing on signs of potential threat overestimated the level of danger.

The final sessions of MCT focused on modifying residual positive and negative metacognitive beliefs. Sadie expressed a common concern about relapsing, but had developed a plan that she was at times implementing. Every other day, she would check her mind for intrusive thoughts in order to ensure that the thoughts had vanished. The counterproductive nature of this strategy was discussed with Sadie and re-conceptualized as a metacognitive belief driving another form of threat monitoring, i.e. "Checking my mind for intrusive thoughts keeps me safe." Modification of this belief was achieved through illustrating that the strategy increased the frequency of thoughts and was a self-initiated trigger for worry. It also played a maintaining role in keeping the sense of threat alive.

A therapy blueprint was developed with Sadie, which comprised a written and diagrammatic representation of the case formulation and an account of how to apply detached mindfulness to intrusive thoughts. Sadie was encouraged to continue to implement the treatment strategies after the end of treatment in order to strengthen her new metacognitive plan with the goal of maintaining and extending the improvement she had made over the course of MCT.

The treatment approach illustrated in this case example has been evaluated in several studies. Wells and Sembi (2004b) treated eight cases in a single case series and Wells et al. (2008) ran an open trial of chronic PTSD cases. In each case, treatment was associated with very large and significant reductions in symptoms, and the majority of patients recovered.

Colbear (2006) reported the results of a randomized controlled trial demonstrating that eight sessions of MCT were highly effective compared to a no-treatment waiting period. In an intention to treat analysis, 80 per cent of the MCT group had recovered (on the Impact of Event Scale) at post-treatment compared with none of the patients in the waiting list condition. In a recent randomized controlled trial, MCT was superior to exposure therapy for PTSD (Proctor, 2008).

# Conclusion

In this book, we have described the theoretical and practical features of MCT and contrasted this approach with other forms of CBT. MCT is based on a specific theory of the control of thinking that leads to persistence and strengthening of psychological disturbance. It provides a distinctive theoretical and clinical approach to understanding and treating psychological disorders, with an emphasis on specific styles of thinking, mental regulation and experiential awareness. The theory is supported by over twenty years of empirical research. Individual treatment techniques and full treatment packages are gaining increasing empirical support (for a review, see Wells, 2009) as effective and efficient interventions.

# References

Arntz, A., Rauner, M. and van den Hout, M. A. (1995). "If I feel anxious there must be danger": Ex-consequentia reasoning in inferring danger in anxiety disorders. *Behaviour Research and Therapy*, 33, 917–925.

Beck, A. T. (1976). *Cognitive Therapy and the Emotional Disorders*. New York: International Universities Press.

Beck, A.T ., Emery, G. and Greenberg, R. L. (1985). *Anxiety Disorders and Phobias: A Cognitive Perspective*. New York: Basic Books.

Beck, A. T., Rush, A. J., Shaw, B. F. and Emery, G. (1979). *Cognitive Therapy of Depression*. New York: Guilford Press.

Borkovec, T. D., Wilkinson, L., Folensbee, R. and Lerman, C. (1983). Stimulus control applications to the treatment of worry. *Behaviour Research and Therapy*, 21(3), 247–251.

Cavanagh, M. and Franklin, J. (2001). Attention training and hypochondriasis: A randomised controlled trial. Paper presented at the World Congress of Cognitive Therapy, Vancouver, Canada.

Clark, D. A. (2004). *Cognitive-Behavioral Therapy for OCD*. New York: Guilford Press.

Colbear, J. (2006). A randomized controlled trial of metacognitive therapy for post-traumatic stress disorder: Post treatment effects. Thesis submitted to the University of Manchester for the degree of Doctor of Clinical Psychology in the Faculty of Medical and Human Sciences.

Dimidjian, S., Hollon, S. D., Dobson, K. S., Schmaling, K. B.,

Kohlenberg, R. J., Addis, M. E., Gallop, R., McGlinchey, J. B., Markely, D. K., Gollan, J. K., Atkins, D. C., Dunner, D. L. and Jacobsen, N. S. (2006). Randomized trial of behavioural activation, cognitive therapy, and antidepressant medication in the acute treatment of adults with major depression. *Journal of Consulting and Clinical Psychology*, 74, 658–670.

Dugas, M. J., Gagnon, F., Ladouceur, R. and Freeston, M. H. (1998). Generalized anxiety disorder: A preliminary test of a conceptual model. *Behaviour Research and Therapy*, 36(2), 215–226.

Ehlers, A. and Clark, D. M (2000). A cognitive model of post-traumatic stress disorder. *Behaviour Research and Therapy*, 38, 319–345.

Ellis, A. (1962). *Reason and Emotion in Psychotherapy*. Secaucus, NJ: Lyle Stuart.

Fisher, P. L. and Wells, A. (2005). Experimental modification of beliefs in obsessive-compulsive disorder: A test of the metacognitive model. *Behaviour Research and Therapy*, 43, 821–829.

Fisher, P. L. and Wells, A. (2008). Metacognitive therapy for obsessive-compulsive disorder: A case series. *Journal of Behavior Therapy and Experimental Psychiatry*, 39(2), 117–132.

Foa, E. B. and Rothbaum, B. O (1998). *Treating the Trauma of Rape: Cognitive Behavioral Therapy for PTSD*. New York: Guilford Press.

Gwilliam, P. D. H., Wells, A. and Cartwright-Hatton, S. (2004). Does metacognition or responsibility predict obsessive-compulsive symptoms? A test of the metacognitive model. *Clinical Psychology and Psychotherapy*, 11, 137–144.

Hanh, T. N. (1976). *The Miracle of Mindfulness: A Manual for Meditation*. Boston, MA: Beacon.

Hayes, S. C., Strosahl, K. D. and Wilson, K. G. (1999). *Acceptance and Commitment Therapy: An Experiential Approach to Behavior Change*. New York: Guilford Press.

Ingram, R. E. and Hollon, S. D. (1986). Cognitive therapy for depression from an information processing perspective. In R. E. Ingram (ed.), *Information Processing Approaches to Clinical Psychology*. Orlando, FL: Academic Press.

Kabat-Zinn, J. (1982). An outpatient program in behavioral medicine for chronic pain patients based on the practice of mindfulness meditation: Theoretical considerations and preliminary results. *General Hospital Psychiatry*, 4(1), 33–47.

Kabat-Zinn, J. (1994). *Wherever You Go, There You Are: Mindfulness Meditation in Everyday Life*. New York: Hyperion.

Kabat-Zinn, J. (1998). Meditation. In J. C. Holland (ed.), *Psycho-oncology*. New York: Oxford University Press.

Leahy, R. L. (2007). Emotional schemas and resistance to change in anxiety disorders. *Cognitive and Behavioral Practice*, 14(1), 36–45.

Masuda, A., Hayes, S. C., Sackett, C. F. and Twohig, M. P. (2004). Cognitive defusion and self-relevant negative thoughts: Examining the impact of a ninety-year-old technique. *Behaviour Research and Therapy*, 42, 477–485.

Mathews, A. and MacLeod, C. (1985). Selective processing of threat cues in anxiety states. *Behaviour Research and Therapy*, 23, 563–569.

Myers, S. G. and Wells, A. (2005). Obsessive-compulsive symptoms: The contribution of metacognitions and responsibility. *Journal of Anxiety Disorders*, 19(7), 806–817.

Myers, S. G., Fisher, P. L. and Wells, A. (2008). Belief domains of the Obsessive Beliefs Questionnaire-44 (OBQ-44) and their specific relationship with obsessive-compulsive symptoms. *Journal of Anxiety Disorders*, 22(3), 475–484.

Nolen-Hoeksema, S. (1991). Responses to depression and their effects on the duration of depressive episodes. *Journal of Abnormal Psychology*, 100, 569–582.

Nolen-Hoeksema, S., Morrow, J. and Fredrickson, B. L. (1993). Response style and the duration of episodes of depressed mood. *Journal of Abnormal Psychology*, 102, 20–25.

OCCWG (1997). Cognitive assessment of obsessive-compulsive disorder. *Behaviour Research and Therapy*, 35(7), 667–681.

OCCWG (2001). Development and initial validation of the obsessive beliefs questionnaire and the interpretation of intrusions inventory. *Behaviour Research and Therapy*, 39, 987–1006.

Papageorgiou, C. and Wells, A. (1998). Effects of attention training on hypochondriasis: A brief case series. *Psychological Medicine*, 28, 193–200.

Papageorgiou, C. and Wells, A. (2000). Treatment of recurrent major depression with attention training. *Cognitive and Behavioral Practice*, 7, 407–413.

Papageorgiou, C. and Wells, A. (2001). Positive beliefs about depressive rumination: Development and preliminary validation of a self-report scale. *Behavior Therapy*, 32, 13–26.

Papageorgiou, C., Wells, A. and Meina, L. J. (in preparation). Development and preliminary evaluation of the Negative Beliefs about Rumination Scale.

Proctor, D. (2008). A randomised controlled trial of metacognitive therapy versus exposure therapy for post-traumatic stress disorder. Thesis submitted to the University of Manchester for the degree of Doctor of Clinical Psychology in the Faculty of Medical and Human Sciences.

Rachman, S. (1997). A cognitive theory of obsessions. *Behaviour Research and Therapy*, 35(9), 793–802.

Roemer, L. and Orsillo, S. M. (2002). Expanding our conceptualization of and treatment for Generalized Anxiety Disorder: Integrating mindfulness/acceptance-based approaches with existing cognitive-behavioral models. *Clinical Psychology: Science and Practice*, 9(1), 54–68.

Roemer, L. and Orsillo, S. M. (2007). An open trial of an acceptance-based behavior therapy for generalized anxiety disorder. *Behavior Therapy*, 38(1), 72–85.

Salkovskis, P. M. (1985). Obsessional-compulsive problems: A cognitive-behavioural analysis. *Behaviour Research and Therapy*, 23, 571–583.

Segal, Z. V., Williams, J. M. G. and Teasdale, J. D. (2002). *Mindfulness-Based Cognitive Therapy for Depression: A New Approach to Preventing Relapse*. New York: Guilford Press.

Siegle, G. J., Ghinassi, F. and Thase, M. E. (2007). Neurobehavioral therapies in the 21st century: Summary of an emerging field and an extended example of cognitive control training for depression. *Cognitive Therapy and Research*, 31, 235–262.

Teasdale, J., Segal, Z. and Williams, J. M. G. (1995). How does cognitive therapy prevent relapse and why should attentional control (mindfulness) training help? *Behaviour Research and Therapy*, 33, 225–239.

Valmaggia, L. R., Bouman, T. K. and Schuurman, L. (2007). Attention training with auditory hallucinations: A case study. *Cognitive and Behavioral Practice*, 14(2), 127–133.

Van Oppen, P. and Arntz, A. (1994). Cognitive therapy for obsessive-compulsive disorder. *Behaviour Research and Therapy*, 32(1), 79–87.

Wells, A. (1990). Panic disorder in association with relaxation-induced anxiety: An attentional training approach to treatment. *Behavior Therapy*, 21, 273–280.

Wells, A. (1995). Meta-cognition and worry: A cognitive model of generalized anxiety disorder. *Behavioural and Cognitive Psychotherapy*, 23, 310–320.

Wells, A. (1997). *Cognitive Therapy of Anxiety Disorders: A Practice Manual and Conceptual Guide*. Chichester: Wiley.

Wells, A. (2000). *Emotional Disorders and Metacognition: Innovative Cognitive Therapy*. Chichester: Wiley.

Wells, A. (2005). Detached mindfulness in cognitive therapy: A metacognitive analysis and ten techniques. *Journal of Rational-Emotive and Cognitive-Behavior Therapy*, 23, 337–355.

Wells, A. (2007). The attention training technique: Theory, effects and a metacognitive hypothesis on auditory hallucinations. *Cognitive and Behavioral Practice*, 14, 134–138.

Wells, A. (2009). *Metacognitive Therapy for Anxiety and Depression.* New York: Guilford Press.

Wells, A. and Cartwright-Hatton, S. (2004). A short form of the metacognitions questionnaire: Properties of the MCQ-30. *Behaviour Research and Therapy*, 42, 385–396.

Wells, A. and King, P. (2006). Metacognitive therapy for generalized anxiety disorder: An open trial. *Journal of Behavior Therapy and Experimental Psychiatry*, 37, 206–212.

Wells, A. and Matthews, G. (1994). Attention and emotion: A clinical perspective. Hove: Erlbaum.

Wells, A. and Matthews, G. (1996). Modelling cognition in emotional disorder: The S-REF model. *Behaviour Research and Therapy*, 34, 881–888.

Wells, A. and Papageorgiou, C. (1998). Social phobia: Effects of external attention on anxiety, negative beliefs and perspective taking. *Behavior Therapy*, 29, 357–370.

Wells, A. and Papageorgiou, C. (2004). Metacognitive therapy for depressive rumination. In C. Papageorgiou and A. Wells (eds), *Depressive Rumination: Nature, Theory and Treatment* (pp. 259–273). Chichester: Wiley.

Wells, A. and Sembi, S. (2004a). Metacognitive therapy for PTSD: A preliminary investigation of a new brief treatment. *Journal of Behavior Therapy and Experimental Psychiatry*, 35, 307–318.

Wells, A. and Sembi, S. (2004b). Metacognitive therapy for PTSD: A core treatment manual. *Cognitive and Behavioural Practice*, 11, 365–377.

Wells, A., Welford, M., Fraser, J., King, P., Mendel, E., Wisely, J., Knight, A. and Rees, D. (2008). Chronic PTSD treated with metacognitive therapy: An open trial. *Cognitive and Behavioral Practice*.

Wells, A., White, J. and Carter, K. (1997). Attention training: Effects on anxiety and beliefs in panic and social phobia. *Clinical Psychology and Psychotherapy*, 4, 226–232.

Wilhelm, S. and Steketee, G. (2006). *Cognitive Therapy for Obsessive-Compulsive Disorder: A Guide for Professionals.* Oakland: New Harbinger Publications.

Williams, J. M. G., Watts, F. N., MacLeod, C. and Mathews, A. (1988). *Cognitive Psychology and Emotional Disorders.* Chichester: Wiley.

# Index